vitality | vīˈtalədē |

noun

- the state of being strong and active; energy: *changes that will give renewed vitality to our democracy.*

- the power giving continuance of life, present in all living things: *the vitality of seeds.*

Oxford English Dictionary, 3rd Ed.

IN THIS ISSUE

LA+ VITALITY
EDITORIAL

Vitality is what the Greeks referred to as the quintessence – the fifth element that catalyzes the other four: earth, water, air, and fire. For science, vitality is latent within matter itself, whereas for religion it is breathed into the clay by a god. Either way, vitality is the elixir and the expression of life, it animated the first cell and it courses through the veins of every living thing to this day. But so what? Why now base a whole issue of LA+ on such a vast and enigmatic theme?

Vitality captures something of the zeitgeist of the Anthropocene – a cultural (and geological) moment characterized by unprecedented knowledge of life's remarkable vitalism on the one hand, and anxiety about its seemingly imminent annihilation on the other. Never before has there been so much human vitality on Earth, and yet this planetary hive of activity now casts the shadow of the sixth extinction. Central to this zeitgeist is humanity's increasing technological ability to manipulate life in all its forms – to breathe vitality into cells, machines, cities, and ecosystems. All of which brings us inexorably back to landscape architecture, for breathing vitality into places is what landscape architects do. In this issue, we've sought to broaden our discipline's thoughts on this task by exploring vitality through multiple disciplinary lenses.

One of the first pieces we sought for this issue is by experimental psychologist Colin Ellard, who explores questions about the roots of our perceptions of life and agency. Recounting his collaborations with artist Phillip Beesley—who creates interactive installations of waving fronds replete with sensors and lights that enthrall audiences with their ambiguously organic and machinic qualities—Ellard builds an argument for urban designers to not only make the city greener and socially more vibrant, but to make cities psychologically more compelling. Alas, this is not what urban designer Julian Bolleter finds in his critical reading of contemporary Dubai. In Bolleter's interpretation, although urban design in Dubai is made to appear vital and inclusive, it is in fact too often a thinly veiled manifestation of autocracy and economic exclusivity replacing once-vibrant and socially complex communities with constructed attractions that reinforce the Dubai "brand." While we can point to Dubai as an extreme case, this frank appraisal of the practices of "placemaking" reminds us that in the name of urban vitality the same techniques are deployed to varying degrees the world over and landscape architects are all too often complicit.

Under the rubric of vitality as a proxy for public health, we explore the boundaries of creating more livable cities with articles by landscape architect Sara Jensen Carr, renowned urban walkability advocate Billie Giles-Corti (with Jonathan Arundel and Lucy Gunn), and landscape historian Mirka Beneš. Related to these, though more personally nuanced, are pieces by Chuan Hao Chen on the metaphor of the medical emergency, and psychiatrist and urban health scholar Mindy Thompson Fullilove on the vitality of main streets in small-town America.

Whereas the research by Bolleter, Jensen Carr, and Giles-Corti and her team are concerned with humanizing the landscapes of growing urban and suburban economies, in articles by designers Christopher Marcinkoski and Clay Gruber we turn to landscapes being drained of socio-economic vitality. Gruber recounts the case study of Tonopah, a former silver-mining town in the high desert of central Nevada, and Marcinkoski describes how he and his students have engaged, in novel ways, with the phenomenon of Tokyo's shrinking population.

In the first of three interviews in this issue, Ellen Neises speaks with Sierra Bainbridge, senior principal at MASS Design Group, whose inspiring health-related work in Rwanda shows how designers can make a meaningful difference to the vitality of rural communities. We also speak with Rob McDonald, lead scientist for Global Cities at The Nature Conservancy, who authored a recent high-profile report, *Nature in the Urban Century*, which features a global assessment of areas crucial to safeguarding biodiversity and human well-being. In casting about for a good example of a city trying to safeguard its biodiversity we asked biologist Andrew Gonzalez to explain his multi-year research into designing a comprehensive and practicable green network for the city of Montreal and its hinterlands.

The third interview in this issue is with Baltimore-based political philosopher Jane Bennett, author of the book *Vibrant Matter*. Bennett argues for the intrinsic vitality and ecological interconnectedness of all matter and in so doing attempts to close down the nature–culture dualism that has bedeviled Western history. Bennett's approach to an ecologically impure world aligns with a new generation of landscape architects, such as Colin Curley who surveys the beautiful ugliness of Newtown Creek, New York's most-polluted waterway. As if his lead character, a human-fish mutant, had crawled out of that very waterbody Jake Boswell then offers a wide-ranging rumination on ecology and aesthetics. And finally, we leave the last word to philosopher Mark Kingwell. He begins his 14-part rumination at the perfect moment to conclude this editorial – the very moment that Dr Frankenstein declares "It's alive! It's alive!"

Richard Weller + Tatum L. Hands
Issue Editors

SARA JENSEN CARR

CORPOREAL ECOLOGIES

Sara Jensen Carr is an assistant professor of architecture, urbanism, and landscape at Northeastern University, and formerly held a joint appointment in the School of Architecture and Office of Public Health Studies at University of Hawaii at Manoa. She was a 2017 Mellon Fellow in Urban Landscape Studies at Dumbarton Oaks, and is currently working on a book for UVA Press titled *The Topography of Wellness: Health and the American Urban Landscape.*

╬ ENVIRONMENTAL STUDIES, PUBLIC HEALTH, URBAN DESIGN

Nature and cities are often conceptualized as opposing forces, the urban condition the cause of illness both actual and existential, and nature as its antidote. Jefferson's *Notes on the State of Virginia* warned the social and political ill effect of cities on American culture "as sores do to the strength of the human body."[1] Others have hypothesized cities as bodies writ large, with landscape as the conduit to its vitality: we can easily envision parks as lungs, walkable streets as circulatory systems, water as lifeblood. That place, and specifically the presence of landscape, shapes well-being seems intrinsic knowledge. Few would dispute the restorative power of contact with nature, but writings from Hippocrates's *Airs, Waters, Places* to Thoreau's *Walden* to Wilson's *Biophilia* have tried to articulate landscape's healing powers. From the Industrial Revolution to the early 1900s, the transformation of the urban landscape was a key factor in eradicating infectious disease. But for the better part of the 20th century, advances in medical practice led to treating internal rather than external causes of ill health. However, as we understand more about the myriad causes of chronic illness, the role of place has once again come under examination as direct and indirect cause. Expanded empirical methods mean that we understand more than ever the effects of our environment on our minds and bodies, but the larger and unanswered question is what we do with this knowledge. In the age of Fitbits, wellness metrics, and smart cities, it is increasingly tempting to quantify "green" as a unit that can be dosed and distributed for maximum efficiency. This data-driven approach may indeed be an effective platform to help people understand the power of urban landscape, but to employ it in this manner is unlikely to improve public health. To understand why, we must look to history and carefully consider the implications of this most recent research.

Arterial Urbanism

Burgeoning factory development and the influx of people to cities during the American and European Industrial Revolutions made sickness palpable in the air and water. An 1858 issue of *Punch* magazine depicts the Grim Reaper rowing a boat on the heavily polluted River Thames, the London skyline behind him, making clear the association between urban development and disease. Industrial waste and rapid development blocked out the sun and clogged rivers and streams. Dirt roads and cobblestone crevices were thought to hold filth that also infected the air above them. Many paths abruptly ended in pools of wastewater and polluted marshland. An 1865 report on the sanitary conditions of New York City contains vivid tactile descriptions of reclaimed ground made of "bricks, mortar, slate, gravel, ashes, coal-dust, street-sweepings, oyster, clam, lobster, and egg shells, pig's hair, shavings, straw, glass, carpets, brooms, refuse materials from tanneries, crockery, bones, dead animals – as cats, rats, and dogs; shoes, boots, feathers, oyster cans, old tin roofs, tin clippings, etc."[2] In most major Western cities, the epidemics of cholera and yellow fever necessitated a partnership between departments of planning and public health, who had little choice but to pave over streams and the ground plane, creating a hardscape that could be washed down and drained.[3]

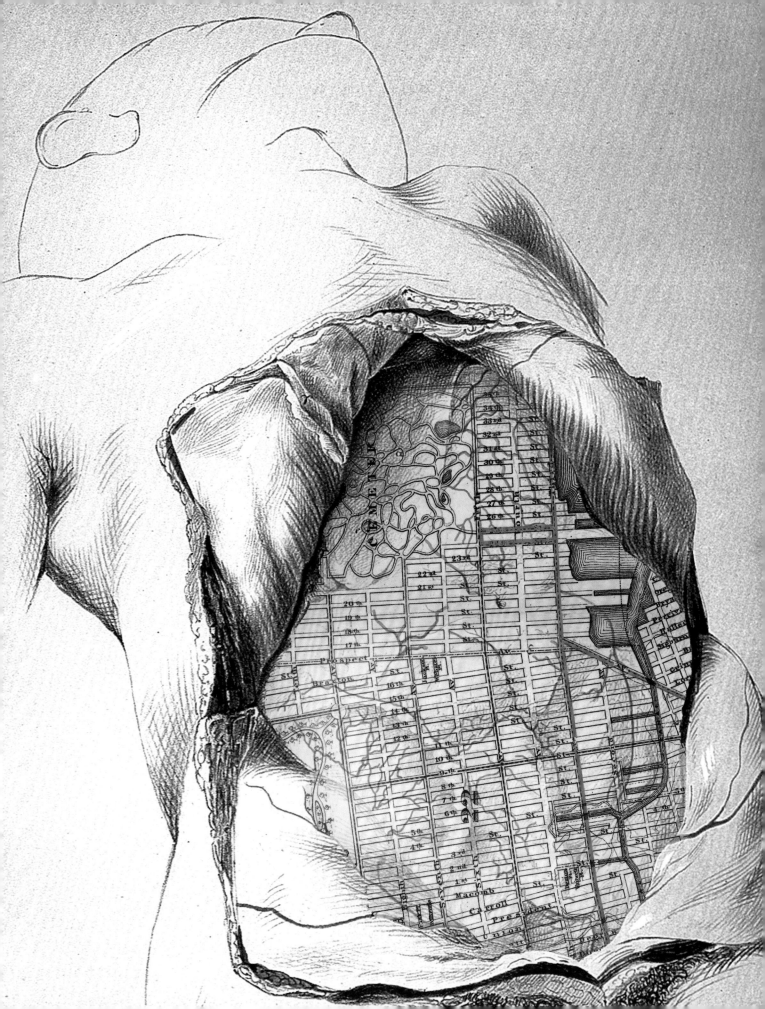

In the Progressive Era (ca. 1870 to 1930), the miasma thought to emanate from the ground and water was largely under control. Frederick Law Olmsted and Daniel Burnham sought to counteract urban density and air pollution by bringing "the nature cure" from the country (where the upper class would escape for fresh air and water) to urban dwellers. The public health platform, particularly given Olmsted's background as a sanitary officer of New York State,[4] gave them the leverage to plan landscapes as pulmonary systems for the city. Physician John Rauch gave medical credence to their designs in his book *Public Parks: Their Effects upon the Moral, Physical and Sanitary Condition of the Inhabitants of Large Cities; With Special Reference to the City of Chicago* (1869), noting specifically the ability of trees to block winds that spread disease, absorb "noxious gases" and produce oxygen.[5] A few decades later, English reformer Ebenezer Howard wrote *Garden Cities of To-morrow* (1902), a utopian town plan outlining prescriptive amounts of green space for recreation and agricultural production per resident, "within 240 yards of the furthest removed inhabitant."[6]

With the advent of germ theory, the partnership between public health and design languished for several decades as predominant infectious diseases could be treated by individualized medical treatment rather than larger environmental interventions. It was the urban crisis of the 1960s and 1970s that gave planners and designers the opportunity to once again seize on health models for design philosophy. Plagues of the built environment–crime, blight, and fire–were granted epidemiological identities and the according remedies took on an increasingly clinical tone, commensurate with a new age of medicine. Geographer Michael Dear used broad contagion metaphors to describe patterns of housing abandonment in Philadelphia[7] while in the 1960s the RAND Corporation advocated for the expansion of urban municipal services to act as "immunization."[8] Even though these afflictions of the urban fabric were born of social and policy environments of racial discrimination and urban disinvestment, they were treated as a virus that simply needed the correct antibiotic. And in the rampant and often disastrous urban renewal projects that often followed, entire neighborhoods (mostly African American) from New York City to New Orleans were eliminated as one would remove a cancerous tumor.[9]

Architects and planners took cues from the increasing exactitude of the medical field, attempting to prescribe landscape as a cure for afflictions of the physical environment and diseases of urban dwellers. The American Planning Association guidelines for green space, which have remained unchanged since 1965, start at one acre per 100 people, and decrease per capita as population rises.[10] Similarly, the World Health Organization recommends 9 m2 per person (approximately one-fifth the APA recommendation). A survey of Le Corbusier's town planning manifestoes describe the compartmentalization and delivery of the environment, undifferentiated from the square footage of a housing unit. In various housing proposals, he dictated 14 m2 per occupant for each unit, 12 m of plate glass window (for proper sun absorption), air to be held at a temperature of 18 degrees Celsius, eight liters of air to circulate the rooms every minute for "exact respiration," and 150 square yards per unit for agriculture.[11] Trees are deployed in straight lines to buffer roads and absorb air pollution but shown planted with acupunctural precision. The aggregate effect, though, is a landscape that is flat, contained, and remote, something to be viewed through the literal orderly frame[12] of a window in a high-rise apartment, placed above the 13th story for "absolute calm and purest air,"[13] and consumed rather than fully occupied.

Dosing the Landscape

Recent research has been able to measure the direct effects of landscape on our health with increased accuracy. For example, Roger Ulrich's study on views of trees from hospital windows and their correlation with faster recovery times effectively kick-started three-plus decades of evidence-based design in the healthcare sector.[14] One of the most studied subjects in health and built environment research has been

1 Thomas Jefferson, *Notes on the State of Virginia* (London: John Stockdale, 1787), 275.

2 *The Slums of New York City: Report of the Council of Hygiene and Public Health of the Citizen's Association of New York upon the Sanitary Conditions of the City* (New York: Appleton, 1865), 196.

3 Jason Corburn, "Reconnecting with Our Roots: American Urban Planning and Public Health in the Twenty-first Century," *Urban Affairs Review* 42, no. 5 (2007): 688; Stanley K. Schultz & Clay McShane, "To Engineer the Metropolis: Sewers, Sanitation, and City Planning in Late-Nineteenth-Century America," *Journal of American History* 65 (1978): 389.

4 Thomas Fisher, "Frederick Law Olmsted and the Campaign for Public Health," *Places Journal*, November 2010, https://doi.org/10.22269/101115 [accessed June 21, 2018].

5 Bonj Szczygiel & Robert Hewitt, "Nineteenth-Century Medical Landscapes: John H. Rauch, Frederick Law Olmsted, and the Search for Salubrity," *Bulletin of the History of Medicine* 74, no. 4 (2000): 726.

6 Ebenezer Howard, *Garden Cities of To-morrow* (London: Swan Sonnenschein & Co., 1902), 24.

7 Michael Dear, "Abandoned Housing," in J. Adams (ed.), *Urban Policy Making and Metropolitan Development* (Cambridge, MA: Ballinger, 1976), 59.

8 Roderick Wallace and Deborah Wallace, "Origins of Public Health Collapse in New York City: The Dynamics of Planned Shrinkage, Contagious Urban Decay and Social Disintegration," *Bulletin of the New York Academy of Medicine* 66, no. 5 (1990): 398.

9 Corburn, "Reconnecting Our Roots," 696; Eric Avila, *The Folklore of the Freeway: Race and Revolt in the Modernist City* (Minneapolis: Quadrant, 2014), 19.

10 American Planning Association. "Standards for Outdoor Recreational Areas," https://www.planning.org/pas/reports/report194.htm [accessed June 21, 2018].

11 Le Corbusier, *Towards a New Architecture* (Mineola, NY: Dover Publications, 1931), 246–51.

12 Joan Iverson Nassauer, "Messy Ecosystems, Orderly Frames," *Landscape Journal* 14, no. 2 (1995): 161. Nassauer posits that landscapes that are robust ecologically are rarely appreciated or maintained.

walkability, specifically the interrelation of urban form and physical activity. A search on the PubMed database employing the terms "health" and "built environment" yielded more than 2,400 results at the time of writing. Other studies have further articulated the connection between landscape and mental health. Frances Kuo and William Sullivan looked at residents with and without views of green space from Chicago's Cabrini-Green projects and the observed effect of landscape on lowering stress, mental fatigue, and violence.[15] Increasingly available neuroscience equipment continues to illuminate our responses to landscape, most notably studies looking at attention restoration in schoolchildren[16] and stress levels in the elderly walking through urban streets and parks.[17] Meanwhile, MIT's Senseable City Lab Treepedia project is tracking the canopy cover of many major cities with an amount of granular detail yet unseen in urban remote mapping and is partnering with the World Economic Forum to start estimating their benefits.[18] To generalize, the body of research is conclusive – landscape in varying forms has wholly positive effects on physical and mental health.

Landscape architects and urban planners gladly welcome the increased field of evidence that points to the importance of their profession, with data serving to unambiguously convince the broader public of its benefits. The research on health and built environment has also driven the production of several design guidelines in the past decade, in which landscape's relevance to well-being is noted, even within buildings. The World Health Organization's *Towards More Physical Activity in Cities*, New York City's *Active Design Guidelines*, and the Active Living Research-funded *Designed to Move: Active Cities* advocate for more trees and parks in general terms, not just to encourage activity but to positively impact mental health. Why, though, when International Well Building Institute outlines "one water feature every 100,000 square feet" and "potted plants or planted beds cover[ing] at least 1% of floor area per floor,"[19] does attaching numbers to landscape come off as arbitrary?

While we can measure landscape with ever more exactitude, it is always going to be a difficult if not impossible proposition to attempt to measure health as a landscape performance issue that can be quantified like gallons of storm-water capture or pounds of carbon sequestered. USDA Forest Service scientists have published a series of rigorously researched and fascinating papers on the economic values of trees, ranging from real estate values to energy savings and infrastructure costs.[20] Even so, when it comes to health value, they remain equivocal, restating the general benefits described above, but unable to attach a dollar value as they have with the other benefits.

As other disciplinary research "discovers" the power of landscape for human health, many outside the profession may see green as a panacea for urban wellness, but the truth is the connection between landscape and well-being is always going to be somewhat of a black box. A major roadblock in funding environmental interventions for health is that while there is an abundance of positive correlative evidence, we have not yet proved causality. However, we must recognize that the environment alone cannot combat epidemics but must be implemented alongside education programs and social support. Perhaps because it complicates the positive effects of landscape, it is often unmentioned in the study on landscape and health that economic status is a primary indicator of well-being, and wealthier neighborhoods often have more trees and parks.[21] To conceptualize "green" as a dosage for our consumption neglects the nuances of designing for place and the wider picture of our own relationship to nature. Outside of Olmsted, many researchers from other disciplines are unaware of historical examples of transforming the urban landscape to improve human health, and while they may see an opportunity to deploy trees and parks with scientific accuracy, reframing the research in the context of history raises alarm. We want to avoid materializing Corbusian landscapes of the midcentury – anemic fields and trees planted acupuncturally from formulas conjured in the "scientific" vacuum. In her essay "The Environment is Not a System," artist and engineer Tega Brain points

13 Le Corbusier, *Towards a New Architecture*, 58.

14 Roger S. Ulrich, "View through a window may influence recovery from surgery," *Science* 224, no. 4647 (1984): 420.

15 Frances E. Kuo & William C. Sullivan, "Environment and Crime in the Inner City," *Environment and Behavior* 33, no. 3 (2001): 360.

16 Dongying Li & William C. Sullivan, "Impact of Views to School Landscapes on Recovery from Stress and Mental Fatigue," *Landscape and Urban Planning* 148, no. C (2016): 149.

17 Peter Aspinall, et al., "The Urban Brain: Analysing Outdoor Physical Activity with Mobile EEG," *British Journal of Sports Medicine* 49 (2015): 275.

18 Senseable City Lab. "Treepedia," http://senseable.mit.edu/treepedia (accessed June 21, 2018).

19 International Well Building Institute, "Biophilia II - Quantitative," https://standard.wellcertified.com/mind/biophilia-ii-quantitative (accessed June 21, 2018).

20 Gregory E. McPherson, "Accounting for Benefits and Costs of Urban Greenspace," *Landscape and Urban Planning* 22, no. 1 (1992): 44; David J. Nowak & John F. Dwyer, "Understanding the benefits and costs of urban forest ecosystems," in J.E. Kuser (ed.) *Urban and Community Forestry in the Northeast* (New York: Springer, 2007), 36.

21 Chona Sister, Jennifer Wolch & John Wilson, "Got Green? Addressing Environmental Justice in Park Provision," *GeoJournal* 75, no. 3 (2010): 243; Jennifer Wolch, John P. Wilson & Jed Fehrenbach, "Parks and Park Funding in Los Angeles: An Equity-Mapping Analysis." *Urban Geography* 26, no. 1 (2005): 17.

22 Tega Brain, "The Environment is Not a System," *A Peer Reviewed Journal About* (2018) http://www.aprja.net/the-environment-is-not-a-system/?pdf=3569 (accessed July 22, 2018).

23 Aldo Leopold, "The Land-Health Concept and Conservation," in *For the Health of the Land: Previously Unpublished Essays and Other Writings* (Washington, DC: Island Press, 1999), 219.

24 Walter B. Cannon, *The Wisdom of the Body* (New York: Norton, 1939), 312–13.

to the tech industry's interest in applying scientific management to environments to combat climate change (specifically, Microsoft's initiative AI for Earth), but rightly points out this has been done in the past, and that the "systems approach" often fails to see complex human interactions and most of all, neglects histories of injustice.[22]

Instead of wielding the research in search of ideal dosages, we should understand it as further articulating the many pathways between landscape and health. Those outside the profession may now expect each tree or square footage of park prove its worth in weight loss, diabetes cases reduced, and dollar amounts of healthcare expenditures is to fundamentally misunderstand urban landscape, and in this era of both environmental and health crises, it will be up to landscape architects to understand and communicate how we can address both issues simultaneously.

Vis mediatrix naturae

The Hippocratic credo *vis mediatrix naturae*, or "nature is the physician of diseases," is often misinterpreted as employing "nature" (landscapes) as a cure, but its original context makes clear the philosopher's hypothesis of the *nature of the human body* to self-regulate for health in the same manner of ecosystems. Ecologist Aldo Leopold also frequently used bodily and wellness metaphors to communicate the importance of environmentalism. In a posthumously published 1946 essay he presciently discusses "the symptoms of disorganization, or land sickness,"[23] including increased flooding, lower crop and forest yields, and sudden outbreaks of pests and disappearances of other species. Conversely, his contemporary, physician Walter B. Cannon, also used ecological metaphors to describe individual and population health, proposing that both naturally seek a state of homeostasis, but the health of the individual is only assured when the larger population is also healthy.[24] Illness in the body, or unexplained catastrophe in a biome, both signal a disruption in these ostensibly self-regulating systems. Interestingly, the consistent theme between Hippocrates, Leopold, and Cannon is that while ecosystems and bodies act in a similar manner, none of them consider their health in relation to each other.

One may point to the burgeoning study of urban metabolism, which does purport to view the city as an ecosystem in search of stability. Curiously, though, for research that uses a bodily metaphor to describe theories of dynamic growth and entropy, they are largely focused on flows of goods, energy, and information, neglecting the thornier issues of human health, environmental justice, and actual urban ecology. Perhaps this is because the challenge of designing to ensure the robustness of people and landscape is always going to transcend economics and resist quantification. Leopold notes that most members of a biome have no numeric value (specifically noting wildflowers and songbirds), yet the entire system depends on them for stability. We rightly venerate Olmsted for so clearly elucidating the connection between public landscape and public health and for making clear the contributions of trees and green space to cleaning the air and water. What often goes unmentioned is that the true value of parks and greenways is when they are accessible to all, uplifting the health of the entire population and particularly those most vulnerable. We must plan our parks, streets, and urban forest not only for maximum return and as units of consumption, but for the widest distribution of equity. This may be the key for the next frontier of health and built environment study. Let us think of urban landscape as catalyst instead of cure. With the growing interest in linking landscape and health, and an ever-expanding field of evidence, it's an ideal time to reframe the inquiry regarding landscape and health by asking larger questions. How do we mutually assure the vitality of urban horticulture, forests, water, and ourselves? How can landscape mediate health inequities driven by economic status? Finally, what is the intertwined epidemiology of ecosystems, cities, and bodies?

THE "SILENT HIGHWAY"-MAN.
"Your MONEY or your LIFE!"

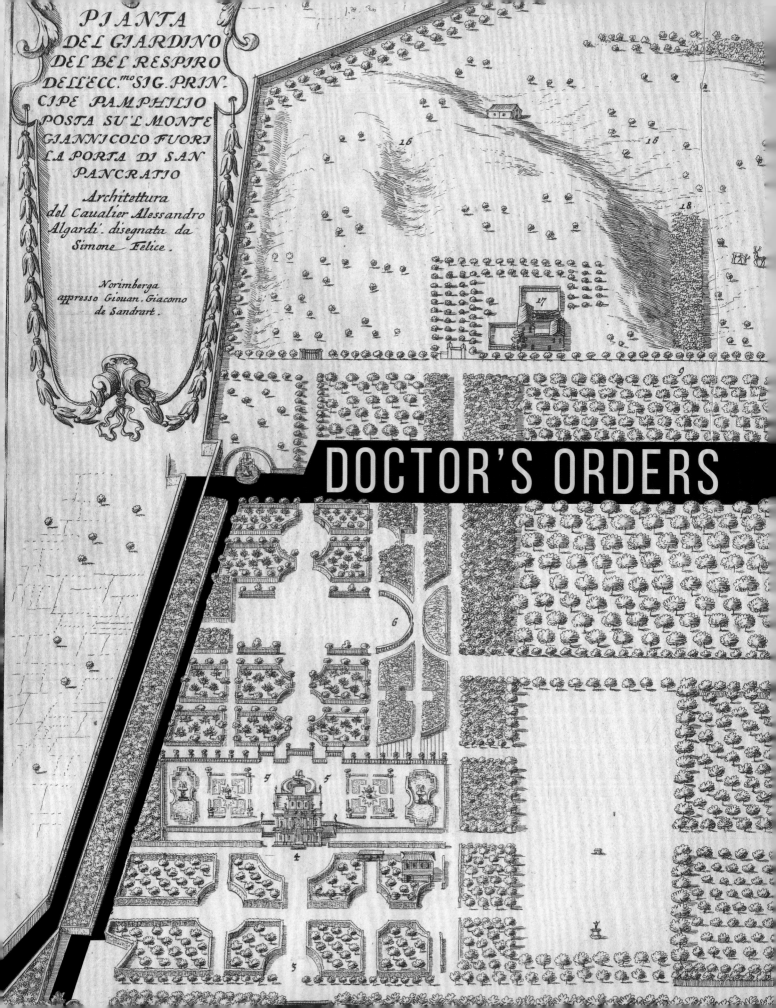

PIANTA
DEL GIARDINO
DEL BEL RESPIRO
DELL ECC.mo SIG. PRIN-
CIPE PAMPHILIO
POSTA SU'L MONTE
GIANNICOLO FUORI
LA PORTA DI SAN
PANCRATIO

Architettura
del Caualier Alessandro
Algardi. disegnata da
Simone Felice.

Norimberga
appresso Giouan. Giacomo
de Sandrart.

DOCTOR'S ORDERS

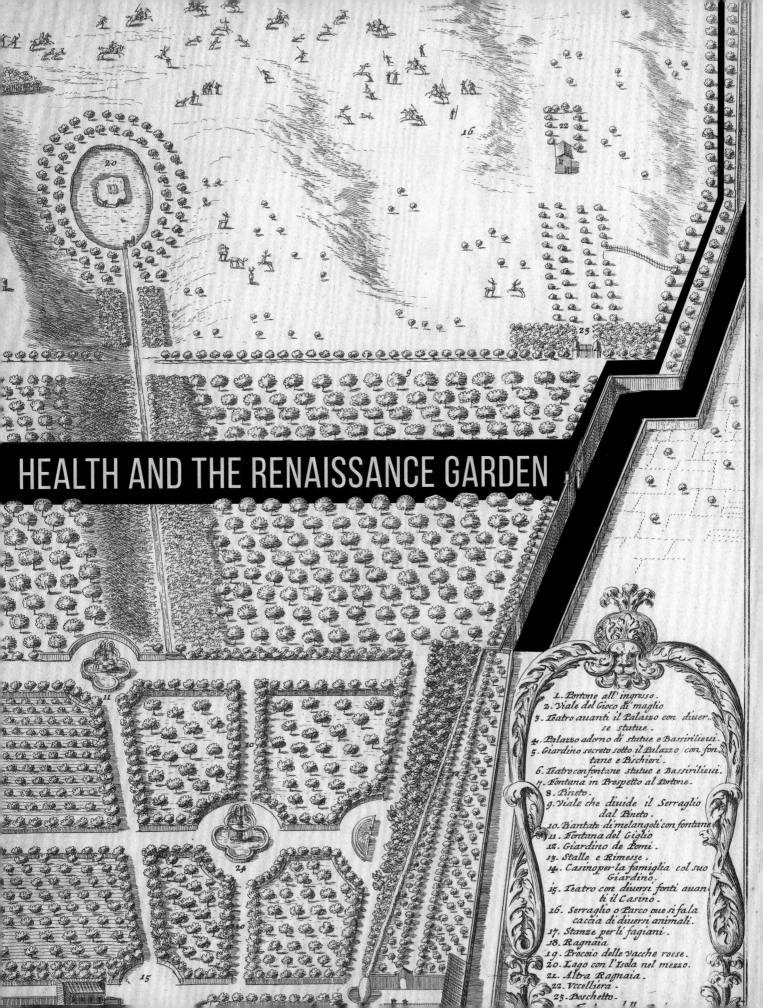

HEALTH AND THE RENAISSANCE GARDEN

1. Portone all' ingresso.
2. Viale del Gioco di maglio
3. Teatro auanti il Palazzo con diuer,, se statue.
4. Palazzo adorno di statue e Bassirilieui.
5. Giardino secreto sotto il Palazzo con fon, tane e Pischieri.
6. Teatro con fontane statue e Bassirilieui.
7. Fontana in Prospetto al Portone.
8. Pineto.
9. Viale che diuide il Serraglio dal Pineto.
10. Piantate di melangoli con fontane
11. Fontana del Giglio
12. Giardino de Pomi.
13. Stalle e Rimesse.
14. Casino per la famiglia col suo Giardino.
15. Teatro con diuersi fonti auan ti il Casino.
16. Serraglio o Parco oue si fa la caccia di diuersi animali.
17. Stanze per li fagiani.
18. Ragnaia.
19. Procoio delle vacche rosse.
20. Lago con l'Isola nel mezzo.
21. Altra Ragnaia.
22. Vccelliera.
23. Boschetto.

MIRKA BENEŠ

Mirka Beneš is an historian of landscape architecture and an associate professor at the
University of Texas at Austin, with a PhD in art
and architectural history from Yale University.
Prior to her appointment at University of Texas,
Beneš taught at Harvard University's Graduate
School of Design for 17 years. Her research and
publications focus on early modern society, villa
gardens, and vernacular and agrarian landscapes
in Rome, and the painter Claude Lorrain.

✚ GARDEN HISTORY, MEDICINE

Both contemporary and historical studies in medicine and design speak repeatedly of "vitality," the moderns citing the visual-mental effect of greenery on "vital organs" and on lowering elevated "vital signs," as well as "creating vital landscapes," and the ancients noting the same effect in ameliorating the flux of "vital spirits" or "vital heat." Both then and now, vitality was a key index of health and also a key result of the often healing experience of nature and gardens.[1] As a historian of landscape architecture, who studies Renaissance Rome and the social and mental experiences of its landscapes and villa gardens, I am inspired by this contemporary research, which has much to teach the historian. And in turn, medical researchers and landscape architects are learning from history; a key player in the field, the landscape architect Catharine Ward Thompson, finds at times "a surprisingly close resonance" between ancient theories and those of today's researchers, concluding that modern psychology usefully confirms historical ideas on mental engagement with landscape.[2]

In this essay, I will pair discussion of contemporary concerns with a case study of health and landscape from mid-17th-century Rome. I will track, using samples from unpublished archival records, the experiences of a Roman noblewoman whose medical reports over 20 years, 1648 to 1668, detail her pathological conditions and the prescriptions by her doctors, which included taking rest in garden settings and taking specific medicines while walking in villas and gardens. This particular female case is seen through the lens of the broader historical picture of health landscapes and that of the medical literature in Renaissance Rome, in which the healthful experience of greenery and gardens was noted by doctors in their treatises. I will begin with, first, a brief historiographical mention of the kind of literature emerging today on health and landscape, and, second, a very brief historical review of landscapes of health and how landscapes over the centuries have been associated with physical and spiritual health. These will provide context for reading the specifics of the historical Roman situation. In the conclusion, I will comment on the "surprisingly close resonance" between past and present perceptions of landscape and health.

While concerned with broad issues of demography, social equity, and sustainability, the current research literature has for some time been structured by a sub-category, namely the healing or therapeutic garden. This now constitutes an entire field of study built on foundational research since the 1990s by the architect and planner Clare Cooper Marcus in the US and the architect Roger S. Ulrich in the US and Sweden. Both have global interests in architecture, landscape architecture, planning, and healthcare, and both have bridged disciplinary boundaries between design and medicine.[3] Much of their research has focused on evidence-based healthcare design in the settings of hospitals, hospices, and convalescent centers, with an emphasis on healing gardens. What statistical and medical evidence, they ask, supports the self-reported or apparent benefits of gardens to health, both physical and mental?

Starting in the late 1970s, Ulrich had pioneered in studying the effects of green scenery and vegetation on human health and vitality, and coined the expression "evidence-based healthcare design," but he was a loner in a field that did not yet exist. This work had a broader context, a generalized return to nature by humans confronting an increasingly urbanizing and industrializing modern world, conceptualized for example in the work of Edward O. Wilson.[4] Foundational works were published by Ulrich, Cooper Marcus, and Wilson from the mid-1990s, and by 2000 the field of therapeutic gardens had taken off. It includes not only gardens in design and experience, but also measuring the salutary experience of gardening and cultivating plants, for example in horticultural therapy.[5] Now, the field is broadening again. Today, landscape architects are increasingly major contributors to the field, and their contributions often center on just how the detailed *designs* of urban green spaces, gardens, and parks work in equilibrating health and vital signs, including through outdoor activity and exercise to combat obesity. For example, Ward Thompson wishes to widen the approach, "to explore engagement with the natural environment in garden, park, and wider landscape as a means to support healthy behaviors and responses."[6]

Health and landscape, natural and designed, have been associated for millennia, whether in the practices of physicians and religious communities or in vernacular culture and folklore. A few key points from ancient, medieval, and modern history of health landscapes can help to situate our Roman Renaissance example.[7] In Roman antiquity, the dialectical notion of the city as unhealthful, crowded, and evil versus the countryside as healthful, restorative, and morally good was expressed in the creation of countless suburban and country villas, replete with gardens for medicinal herbs and for exercise, including pools for swimming and cooling. That dialectic has endured for centuries, even in Central Park, New York, and its progeny. Evoking the authority of Greek doctors, Vitruvius, the Roman architect writing around 15 BCE, proclaimed in his *Ten Books on Architecture* that green surroundings and exercise had beneficial effects on the human body and mind. Many architects should study medicine, he advocated. And he noted a direct causal relationship between exercise, viewing greenery, the air that [he thought] emanated from plants, and ophthalmological health: "Walking in the open air is very healthy, particularly for the eyes, since the refined and rarefied air that comes from green things, finding its way in because of physical exercise... leaves the sight keen."[8]

Much of Hippocrates's thought bequeathed to the Byzantine, Islamic, and medieval European worlds, including his tract on *Airs, Waters, and Places*, stressed climate, water quality, and a beautiful landscape environment for good health.[9] In Medieval Europe and the Islamic East, medicine, food, plants, and gardens went hand in hand, fed by Greek medical tracts translated into Arabic and then into Latin. These pointed to the many roles that flowering plants and their perfumes had in the health of body

1 Magdalena van den Berg, et al., "Visiting Green Spaces is Associated with Mental Health and Vitality: A Cross-Sectional study in Four European Cities," *Health & Place* 38 (2016): 8–15.

2 Catharine Ward Thompson, "Linking Landscape and Health: The Recurring Theme," *Landscape and Urban Planning* 99, no. 3 (2011): 187–95, at 187.

3 See, e.g., Roger S. Ulrich, "Evidence-Based Health-Care Architecture," *The Lancet* 368 (2006): 538–39.

4 Edward O. Wilson, *Biophilia* (Cambridge, MA: Harvard University Press, 1984).

5 Key studies include Roger S. Ulrich, "Visual Landscapes and Psychological Well-Being," *Landscape Research* 4, no. 1 (1979): 17–23; Roger S. Ulrich, "View Through a Window May Influence Recovery from Surgery," *Science* 224, no. 4647 (1984): 420–21; Ulrich, et al., "A Review of the Research Literature on Evidence-Based Healthcare Design," *HERD* 1, no. 3 (2008): 61–125; Clare Cooper Marcus & Marni Barnes (eds), *Healing Gardens: Therapeutic Benefits and Design Recommendations* (New York, NY: John Wiley, 1999). Of equal importance in the development of this research field, focused on case studies, is the collaborative work of a landscape architect, a physician, and an urban historian: Nancy Gerlach-Spriggs, Richard Enoch Kaufman & Sam Bass Warner Jr, *Restorative Gardens: The Healing Landscape* (New Haven: Yale University Press, 1998). For research by psychologists on therapeutic gardening, with a large bibliography, see Jane Clatworthy, Joe Hinds & Paul M. Camic, "Gardening as a Mental Health Intervention: A Review," *Mental Health Review Journal* 18, no. 4 (2013), 214–25. This aspect is also related to the large current field of urban agricultural studies.

6 Ward Thompson, "Linking Landscape and Health," 187–88; also see Catherine Ward Thompson, Peter Aspinall & Simon Bell (eds), *Innovative Approaches to Researching Landscape and Health. Open Space: People Space* 2 (London: Routledge, 2010).

7 A comprehensive documentary history of health and landscape, including healing gardens, is yet to be written. For the earlier periods, see the excellent account in Carole Rawcliffe, "'Delectable Sightes and Fragrant Smelles': Gardens and Health in Late Medieval and Early Modern England," *Garden History* 36, no. 1 (2008): 3–21. Fine overviews, mostly on the modern period, are in Gerlach-Spriggs, et al., *Restorative Gardens*, 7–32; Karen R. Jones, "'The Lungs of the City': Green Space, Public Health and Bodily Metaphor in the Landscape of Urban Park History," *Environment and History* 24 (2018), 39–58. Also see Cooper Marcus & Barnes, Healing Gardens, 1–26 and Ward Thompson, "Linking Landscape and Health," 188–93.

8 Several of the new studies published today on health and landscape cite or begin with Vitruvius. The quotation from Vitruvius, *The Ten Books on Architecture*, Bk 5.9.5, is from Jones, "The Lungs of the City," 43–44.

9 Ward Thompson, "Linking Landscape and Health," 188–89; Rawcliffe, "Delectable Sightes and Fragrant Smelles," 3–21.

10 Rawcliffe, ibid, 6: "Whereas foul odors (miasmas) were believed to spread sickness, floral perfume, fresh air and a verdant landscape helped to prevent it by promoting physical and mental stability."

11 Ibid, 8.

12 See the essays in D. Fairchild Ruggles (ed.), *Sound and Scent in the Garden* (Washington, DC: Dumbarton Oaks Research Library and Collection, 2017).

13 Cited in Cooper Marcus & Barnes, *Healing Gardens*, 12.

14 See Frances Gage, "Chasing 'Good Air' and Viewing Beautiful Perspectives: Painting and Health Preservation in Seventeenth-Century Rome," in Sandra Cavallo & Tessa Storey (eds), *Conserving Health in Early Modern Culture. Bodies and Environments in Italy and England* (Manchester, England: Manchester University Press, 2017), 237–61.

15 The medical records, dating ca. 1648–68, are kept with documents relating to the marriage in 1646 of Olimpia and Camillo Pamphilj, in the Archivio Doria-Pamphilj, Rome: Scaffale 93/57/2, subinterno 51, no. 1, "Ragguaglio de' mali patiti dall' ecc.(ellentissi) ma Signora cavato da consulti, che appresso di me si trovano del s.re Antonio Maria de Rossi per molti anni indietro, e poi da discorsi fatti da Signori Medici, c'hora mi servono." (Account of the ills suffered by the most excellent Lady, drawn from consultations, which are in my possession, of Antonio Maria de Rossi, going back many years, and then from advice given by doctors who now serve her). Translations are the author's. See for the quotations that follow here, fols. 1r-v, 2v, 3r, and 5v.

16 For new research on medical advice on outdoor exercise for men and women in Renaissance Italy, also with respect to villa gardens, see Susan Russell, "The Villa Pamphilj on the Janiculum Hill: The Garden, the Senses and Good Health in Seventeenth-Century Rome," in Alice E. Sanger & Siv Tove Kulbrandstad Walker (eds), *Sense and the Senses in Early Modern Art and Cultural Practice* (Farnham, Surrey, England-Burlington, VT: Ashgate, 2012), 129–46; Sandra Cavallo & Tessa Storey, "Healthy, 'Decorous' and Pleasant Exercise: Competing Models and the Practices of the Italian Nobility (Sixteenth to Seventeenth Centuries)," in Rebekka von Mallinckrodt & Angela Schattner (eds), *Sports and Physical Exercise in Early Modern Culture: New Perspectives on the History of Sports and Motion* (Surrey, England: Ashgate, 2016), 165–88.

17 Girolamo Mercuriale, *De Gymnastica* (Venice, 1569), Book v, ch. xii. Girolamo Mercuriale, *De Arte Gymnastica*, critical edition by C. Pennuto (ed.) and V. Nutton (trans.) (Florence: Olschki, 2008), 599.

18 Such efforts are evident in current research, as in Danya Kim and Jangik Jin, "Does Happiness Data Say Urban Parks are Worth It?," *Landscape and Urban Planning* 178 (2018): 1–11.

and mind through scent and sight."[10] Herbals (medical texts on plants) abounded, and most medieval monasteries and convents had porticoed cloister gardens for healthful walking in inclement weather, as well as medicinal herb gardens, the *herbaria*. Sight and taste (meaning diet) were as important as scent.

Following the Greeks Hippocrates and Galen, medieval and Renaissance doctors used a medical framework based on the four humors (heat, cold, moisture, and dryness), which the human being had to balance constantly, if precariously. What was eaten was understood to be transformed into a warm substance emitted by the heart into the body, called *pneuma* or vital spirit.[11] The vital spirit could ultimately be animated by the multivalent impact of gardens on both the human physiological and psychological states through sight, scent, and taste, and also hearing and touch.[12] The enduring knowledge of the healthful roles of gardens and greenery was incorporated from the 18th through the 20th centuries in specialized healthcare facilities that included gardens or even parkland. These sites operated on both fronts: preventative and curative-therapeutic of ill health. If we read the words of an important late 18th-century German theorist of garden art, Christian Cay Lorenz von Hirschfeld, on what a hospital garden should be, we sense how little has changed since then in the essentials that such gardens bring: "Because a view from the window into blooming and happy scenes will invigorate the patient, also a nearby garden encourages patients to take a walk."[13]

These landscapes of health provide the backdrop against which we can situate an interesting case study of the Roman noblewoman, Princess Olimpia Aldobrandini (1623–1682), grandniece of Pope Clement VIII. The setting is the city of papal Rome—ruled by elected monarchs, the popes—and its villas and countryside in what we can call the long Renaissance, ca. 1400 to 1750. Rome's villas and gardens, whether Villas Giulia and Medici in town or Villa d'Este in the countryside at Tivoli, are famous since centuries, and their forms have been well studied by historians in terms of ownership, architecture, decoration, and planting design. Far less well known are the functions and, especially, the emotional, sensorial, and medical perceptions of Roman gardens. Gardens were thought to both maintain and restore health by balancing the four humors and activating the senses: touch and movement in walking, climbing stairs, and feeling cold water on one's hands or face; smelling and tasting plants and fruits; hearing the captivating and restful sounds of birdsong and gurgling and spraying waters in fountains; and seeing the color green in foliage and trees, order in well-designed gardens, and soft forms in pastoral, idyllic rural landscapes – all good for the health of eyes and mind. Our word "recreation" comes from the Renaissance Italian *ricrearsi* (and its Latin origin, *recreare*), to create oneself anew, which was then very much used with respect to gardens. In general, gardens and their avenues for walking were recognized as healthier and cleaner environments than city spaces, since streets and piazzas in urban Renaissance Rome, as elsewhere in Europe, hosted refuse from houses, detritus from daily markets, and at times raw sewage.

Health and landscape had a particularly symbiotic resonance in Olimpia's time, because Italians were obsessed with their health and they had such close connections to landscape, first, through their daily lives in Italy's fertile and beautiful landscapes and, second, as farm and garden owners therein. The obsession was justified, given how precarious life was due to illness, plague, death in childbirth, and social violence and war. In papal Rome, sorties from the city to the suburbs and the hill towns around Rome for recreation and rest in the healthful gardens of villas and smaller properties took place in a seasonal cycle: in summer the papal court vacated the Vatican (*vacatio*, source of the word, vacation) and withdrew from Rome to countryside properties or to gardens on the hills of Rome, deemed healthful for their better air and breezes. Recent research has shown how frequently Romans who could afford it moved about, in search of drier or wetter air, depending on the individual composition of their humoral balances.[14]

Olimpia Aldobrandini's case is particularly fascinating and her surviving health records are precious documents, since medical records of women in Renaissance Rome are rarely found, as women held lesser roles in society (even when high-born) than men. Rome's population around 1600 counted one third women and two-thirds men, and medicine in Renaissance Italy was a man's world, with medical treatises and health advice books written by men for men. Most studies to date have focused on the advice-literature of how-to books on medicine, diet, and exercise such as hunting, and few consider private medical records, which allow us to see what was prescribed as well as the outcomes, good or bad. During her life in Rome, Olimpia was attended by several physicians, and by one in particular, a renowned doctor named Antonio Maria de Rossi 1588–1671), physician to her granduncle Pope Clement VIII (d. 1605) and student of the even more famous physician, Girolamo Mercuriale (1530–1606).[15] Married at age 15, Olimpia had 10 children by two husbands, difficult pregnancies, and many miscarriages, a situation typical of women whose role it was to provide progeny for the family line of their husbands. Her doctors' notes reveal much sympathy and compassion for her. Some relief from the fevers, corporeal swelling, fainting, and tremendous melancholia that accompanied each pregnancy for months came from the walks and rest that her doctors prescribed she take in the Roman villa gardens and at her own Villa Aldobrandini at Frascati.

After her eighth child was born in April 1653, not even these prescriptions helped: as her doctor noted, "she had such great melancholy, that she said she would have killed herself if she had been alone," adding that "on June 1st she was carried out to Frascati, where she remained for 14 days, doing a (laxative) purge, but not being liberated of her illness. Returning to Rome, since she began to have fainting spells...she continued the purge...and took medicines while walking in the Villa of Prince Ludovisi. That promenade did not go so happily; in fact, instead she began to feel heaviness in the stomach, anxiety, fainting spells, thirst, headache, and redness in the face." Ten years

later, her doctor reported that she had somewhat improved in health, because for the preceding five years she had been taking donkey's milk as a remedy, "but it was necessary that she drink it in the villa, away from any worry, for when she was in the city, moving only about her house, [she became ill again]." The city represented threat of illness, while the countryside retreat, being "in villa," represented recreation, exercise, and connection to the vitality of nature.

Following the recommendations in his teacher's treatise on health and exercise, the *De Gymnastica* (1569) by Girolamo Mercuriale, Olimpia's doctor recommended resting and light exercise, especially walking in gardens. Mercuriale, like other physicians of his time, felt that *moto* or movement was essential in balancing the humors and that such exercise for women should be limited to swinging in a swing (say, from a tree), riding in a carriage, which provided motion, or walking.[16] Men, instead, were encouraged to walk, fence, play ball games, and hunt as exercise. Citing the authority of ancient physicians and Vitruvius, whom he much admired, Mercuriale had advised that all exercises such as walking in the open air were preferable to those performed in a portico: "Walking in the open is also heartily commended by Vitruvius, especially if there are green shades: they are, says he, extremely healthy, especially for the eyes."[17] The approach was a holistic one: not only would movement shake up Olimpia's presumably imbalanced four humors of hot, cold, dry, and wet, but in the process the beneficial effects of seeing greenery in a garden, would aid her recovery. The lengthy report ends in 1668 with the opinions of several doctors that her best chances to maintain her health, after decades of a debilitating life, would come from, "first, for the dietetics (hygienic) part, which consists of the good regimen of the six non-natural things [of Galen], the air is primary, which should be clear, benign, and healthy, and of that kind, as the air of Frascati." As well, she should take frequent exercise on foot or in carriage; in fact, after carriages were introduced to Rome from northern Europe in the later 16th century, Roman patricians took to promenading by carriage in their estate villas. And finally, her doctors prescribed that she should keep taking "the usual powder composed of daisies, powdered horn of the stag, and ground ivory," while on serene days taking the air in her urban garden on the Quirinal hill in Rome, "where her movements should be moderate so as not to agitate her and heat up her humors."

The villa gardens in which Olimpia Aldobrandini carried out her doctors' orders, according to her medical records, were, besides her small urban garden just mentioned, the large ones of her own Villa Aldobrandini at Frascati (built ca. 1600) and the Villas Borghese and Ludovisi on the Pincian hill in Rome (built in the 1620s), which belonged to other Roman noble families. They were all sited atop hills, where healthful breezes could rally weakened "vital spirits," and where Olimpia could find the best air. They were large estates, measuring from 500 meters by a kilometer to a kilometer by 1.5 kilometers. They were subdivided in parts, with one third to one half planted as formal tree gardens – vast stands of umbrella pines, firs, laurel, and bitter orange trees, in separate blocks by species. The remainder was designed as open parkland with meadows, groves of trees, and in the case of Villa Borghese, a hunting park and a lake, as at the Villa Pamphilj (built 1640s–1670s) on the Janiculum hill in Rome. With long avenues bordered by rows of trees, they provided the walkways and ample greenery prescribed by the doctors. If we compare them with the modern tradition of the healing garden, we note immediately that the Roman gardens were not specialized healing gardens, but rather multi-functional gardens, created to display collections of ancient sculpture and rare plants, like outdoor museums, to provide recreation through walks and contact with waterworks, to provide food such as the candied oranges made from the bitter orange trees, to represent the status and cultivation of their owners, to entertain guests, and to provide for healthful green settings.

In concluding, we return to the "surprisingly close resonance" that Ward Thompson and several other researchers have found between ancient and contemporary approaches to the prophylactic, health-maintaining, and curative abilities of landscape architecture. They point to the need to gain further understanding of the causal mechanisms between landscape and health. Studying historical cases in cultural context will allow us to follow the threads of those mechanisms in slow motion, as it were, refining our understanding of the physical and cultural web in which evidence of health benefits is suspended. We can then transpose to the present such methodologies from analyzing the past. And this may help us in evidence-based research, enriching our methods of quantifying evidence that regards the quality of life and experience.[18]

CHUAN HAO CHEN
HABITS OF VITALITY

Chuan Hao (Alex) Chen is an MD-PhD candidate in anthropology at the University of Pennsylvania. He holds a Bachelor of Architecture from Cornell and a Masters of Design from the Harvard Graduate School of Design. His research engages the intersection of culture, health, and design, using ethnographic and design methods to elucidate and speculate upon the cultural construction of healthcare spaces and infrastructure.

✚ PUBLIC HEALTH, MEDICINE, DESIGN

I recently volunteered for an experiment at the University of Pennsylvania School of Nursing that involved virtual reality (VR) and emergency response. The research assistant, who hunted all over the library for study participants, explained that they wanted to simulate an event and observe how people would act. She made me put on some heavy black goggles and I found myself standing on the sidewalk of a crudely drawn 3D city. I watched passersby wander around the streets aimlessly, sometimes walking straight into me and disappearing from sight. A few seconds later, a man came into my view from the left. As soon as he walked in front of me, he collapsed.

Before putting on the VR goggles, I had guessed (because this was a nursing school study) that the simulated scenarios would be medical: perhaps involving someone getting injured or someone collapsing and becoming unresponsive. These are the typical scenarios in basic life support (BLS) training taught to healthcare providers like nurses and doctors, but especially emergency medical technicians (EMTs). As I signed the research consent form, I frantically tried to recall the BLS skills that I had learned during my EMT training, scared that I would not remember what to do in case I do encounter a medical emergency in real life. I learned BLS because knowing how to save a life seems important, especially when the chances of someone choking or having a heart attack in a contemporary city is very real and there are concrete interventions.

As soon as the man collapsed, I fell into BLS mode and started the steps for cardiopulmonary resuscitation (CPR), a part of the BLS protocol. I crouched down on the floor to check for his response. "Sir, sir, are you alright? Are you okay?" Given that this was a visual simulation, I was surprised to feel a three-dimensional head and torso where I saw the downed man on the screen. I first checked for a pulse by touching his neck, then I crouched down to see if his chest rose and fell with each breath. Being a mannequin, the man had neither signs of life. I shouted at one of the wandering bystanders to get help, and to my surprise he responded by pulling out his phone. I started doing chest compressions, pushing in order to help his stilled heart pump blood. The familiar sensation of silicon skin triggered my memory: "One, two, three, four…" I counted out the compressions, screaming into what I knew was an empty seminar room in the library. After 20 pushes, I tilted his head back to deliver two breaths via mouth-to-mouth resuscitation. Perhaps recognizing my hesitation at putting my mouth on a mannequin without a protective mask, the research assistant spoke, "It's okay, just go through the motions, you don't have to actually do it." I hovered my mouth over the patient's mouth and blew. I then returned to chest compressions, and the research assistant stopped me after three more rounds of CPR.

The purpose of the study was to see how many people know how to act in a medical emergency. While we can always call 911, every second counts in these scenarios. Having someone close by who can start CPR before the professionals arrive increases the patient's chance of survival. They also wanted to see how VR technology could help people learn and practice for such scenarios.

From a systems perspective, this problem seems technical. The task is to figure out how to put people with the right skills in the right space at the right time. But it's hard to account for the impact of emotions—of fear and exhilaration—when you literally hold another's life in your hands. I felt the sweat bead up around my forehead and my heart sink into my stomach in a rush of adrenaline as soon as I saw the man collapse in front of me. These fight or flight symptoms are not just for the patient whose life is hanging in the balance: they are experienced by both everyday and professional rescuers.

Because these physical symptoms and emotions make it difficult for rescuers, especially novices, to focus on their task, training programs stress the importance of muscle memory. In an emergency situation, there is no time to think or to process one's own emotions. Repeated practice habituates rescuers, making their life-saving skills a banal reflex. During the experiment, this embodied memory helped me recall how to properly perform CPR. I remembered that compression forces came from the hips and not the arms, where I needed to use my pelvis as a hinge to exert more pressure.

In Elaine Scarry's "Thinking in an Emergency,"[1] she speaks of the heart having "forgotten" how to pump life-sustaining blood to the rest of the body. The EMT's muscle memory remembers for the patient's heart, and he or she works to pump in place of the patient's heart. The amount of energy required to push blood throughout the patient is not trivial: every ounce of energy helps to perfuse vital organs with essential oxygen and nutrients. Pushing hard is an act of transferring the rescuer's vitality, their own life forces, into the patient. Such transfers of energy need to be habitual, a life-saving reflex, and this is the first meaning of what I think of as "habits of vitality." It is a physical act of transference.

But if reflex depends on the consistency of the trigger impulses—like seeing someone collapse on the street—in order to produce the same response, then space becomes another variable that needs to be made consistent between training and practice. A different environment would not trigger the same reflex. VR simulation would get the trainee as close as possible to a projected future scenario. The hustle and bustle of the city and the feeling of being surrounded by buildings and bystanders are all potential distractors that may prevent the activation of muscle memory. Simulation allows trainees to normalize these experiences, so they can focus on the task at hand, rescuing the patient. VR turns the unexpected into routine and makes possible the reflexive habits of saving a life.

While VR brings spatial experience into training spaces, EMTs also actively reproduce the spaces in which they learned their habits: the safety of the classroom. EMTs have a term, "scene safety," which refers to the importance of assessing dangers in the environment. Rushing into an unsecured area could turn rescuers into patients, necessitating even more emergency response resources. Rather than confronting the unknown, EMTs, working with police and others, make sure that the environment conforms to the same safety that they've been habituated to in the classroom.

In *The Production of Space*, Henri Lefebvre highlighted three critical dimensions: representational space, representations of space, and spatial practice.[2] It is spatial practice that is salient here, allowing us to conceptualize vitality as a practiced production of space. The emergency responder's body dialectically negotiates the space of practice with actual scenes of emergency. Their body is the link between these two spaces. Practice, the lived experience, also helps us move beyond thinking of space as merely containers for human activity. On a bodily scale, CPR is an intensely spatial and physical phenomenon that pushes blood throughout the body. Spaces, in the sense of the environment external to the body, also initiate habits of vitality. VR simulates future spaces so emergency rescuers can "remember" their training in a similar future scenario. Conversely, EMTs reproduce the places in which they practice, actively making sure that the space is as safe as the classrooms in which they formed their physical habits of vitality.

Such reproduction of space is also habitual, the repetition of the sensation of creating space. Even as the environment may trigger muscle memory, there's a moment during CPR in which emergency rescuers push out all senses of the world in order to focus on the patient. The edges of one's vision become blurred as the patient comes to dominate the field of vision. One also feels nothing except for increasing muscle fatigue and the way the patient's body resists the compression. Rib cages are designed to protect vital organs from precisely such physical intrusions, and one devotes their entire attention to the act of compression itself. I think of the creation of this experiential space as spatial habits of vitality, conjured and reconjured during emergency rescue.

Slowly, with each practice, emergency rescuers form these muscle memories and spatial habits of vitality. Each instance in a creation of that space, an experiential moment of attending to and focusing on the patient's body. Both obviation of the *mis-en-scène* and feeling the heft or corporality of the life in front of you are dimensions of this space of emergency rescue. Within that realm, there is a bonding between the patient and the rescuer, a bond that allows for the transfer of vitality. There is also the bonding of past and present through memory.

Yet it is also a moral commitment to keep someone alive. This is the third habit of vitality, an ethical recognition of the importance of life. One can learn the "techniques of the body,"[3] but one also needs to learn the impulse and imperative to physically attend to the dying. This is more than the cognitive understanding that life is important, which most would probably share. The issue is that such mental understandings do not necessarily translate into action. This is not meant as a critique of hypocrisy, but rather to highlight the importance of practice to turning theoretical ethics into its embodied actualization. Heroes of emergency rescue were not born with life-saving impulses; they were habituated into them. With each production of lived space, there is a concomitant production of ethical space, one in which we focus on the preservation of vitality.

Whether in the classroom, in virtual reality, or on the streets of a city, recursive formations of habits of vitality affirm the centrality of life to the production of space. This ethical production of space is a social process whereby multiple agents become responsive to and responsible for one another needs. On the surface, emergency response seems like a technical challege of getting EMTs to patients as fast as possible. However, Good Samaritan laws and widespread first aid training among nonprofessionals who often reach the patient first, demonstrate that it's not just a professional problem. For emergency medical systems to be responsive and flexible in myriad unpredictable situations, everyday laypersons should be given the tools to help one another. Habits of vitality can be cultivated by anyone and everyone in order to develop true resilience.

What can emergency response and BLS/CPR tell us about the design of spaces, especially where it concerns the cultivation of habits of vitality? George McKay has written about "radical gardening" and its importance as political statements and "social experiments that invert our positive expectations of the human exchange that occurs in the green open space of a garden."[4] He calls practices like victory gardens, hippie flower protests, and Banksy's masked rioters throwing flowers, "horticountercultural politics."[5] The garden is the locus of a host of global concerns, and it becomes a site of both symbolic resistance and material intervention. Landscapes can help us practice political habits of vitality.

In the history of capital, it was the control and regulation of land, the space of agricultural production, that initiated the increasing gap between the haves and have nots. The enclosures—fencing in of grazing land meant for the public—separated people from their livelihoods. Livelihood in this sense meant more than the making of money; it meant cultivating the relationship between humans and non-humans, of mutual ecological interdependence. The separation of commons was more than the division of space: it cut people off from their everyday interactions with plants and animal species.

Like CPR, agriculture is a recursive activity that transfers the farmer's vital energy into other lives, through similar mechanisms of bodily memory. From sunup to sundown, the acts of watering, weeding, removing pests, and harvesting establish an intimate connection and space in which what matters is the responsibility of each lifeform to the other. The proverbial "green thumb" is the horticultural equivalent of "push harder." These skills are not innate to particular individuals, they are developed through repetition. Experience is what makes the successful farmer or gardener. In turn, the cared-for species nourish human life. They engage dialectically.

Design methodologies that consider habits of vitality move discourses of sustainability beyond that of technical problem-solving. Interventions are historical processes that occur through time, not one-time changes in form that automatically produce the desired results. The implementation of solar energy, for example, requires the gradual familiarization of people to the technology and their incorporation into everyday living. Time is a productive area for design and sociological intervention.

The lessons of enclosure provide another fruitful rethinking of ecological design, one that would decenter human needs and consider instead the mutual reliance of disparate life forms. To invert enclosure is to re-establish connections. Construction of coastal wetlands, for example, are not simply technological solutions to the problem of coastal flooding. They entail a new engagement with wetland species, one that considers their needs, habits, and practices, in order to sustain them. Anthropocentric modernist "machines for living" did not adequately account for the flourishing of botanical lives within their concrete cracks: habits of vitality demand constant engagement.

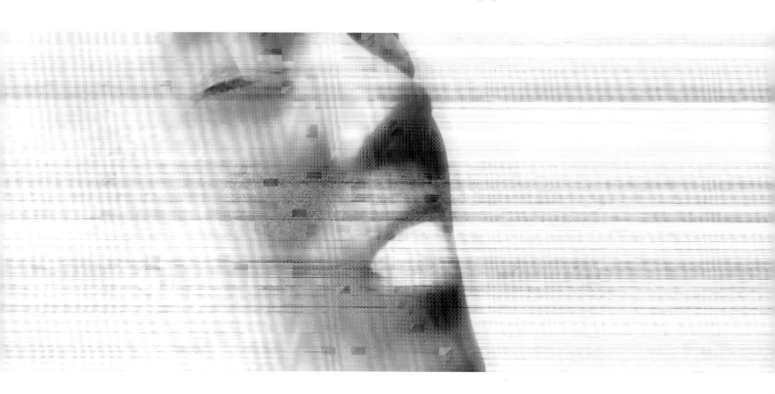

The challenge is to think about how relationships between species are formed and strengthened through recursive contact in order to come to a new way of living with each other. Resilient systems depend on this flexibility, a kind of mutual formation of habits that work for one another. Moreover, habits of vitality entail the repeated production of ethical social spaces that democratize expert thinking. Participatory design creates the space for people to bring in their own habits and experience, expertise, into the formation and address of common problems. Just as resilient medical systems cannot be sustained by the training of EMTs alone—they need also to include the everyday Samaritan—design cannot be conducted just by professional designers, especially if designs are meant to last.

Dialectically, this also means that everyday individuals must step beyond the division of labor which abdicates our mutual responsibility for each other to expert knowledge. The courage to rush to the patient's side is needed outside of medicine. Landscapes are spaces that are constituted by human and non-human commitments to each other's vitality. How do we reconsider, then, our refamiliarization with each other's life cycle, niche, and needs? What alternative habits of vitality can we cultivate for a more productive future?

1 Elaine Scarry, *Thinking in an Emergency* [New York: W.W. Norton & Co., 2012].

2 Henri Lefebvre, *The Production of Space*, trans by Donald Nicholson-Smith [Oxford: Blackwell, 1991].

3 Marcel Mauss, "The Notion of Body Techniques," in *Sociology and Psychology: Essays* [London: Routledge & Kegan Paul, 1970], 95–119.

4 George McKay, "Radical Plots: The Politics of Gardening," *The Independent* [May 2, 2011], https://www.independent.co.uk/property/gardening/radical-plots-the-politics-of-gardening-2277631.html [accessed August 1, 2018].

5 Ibid.

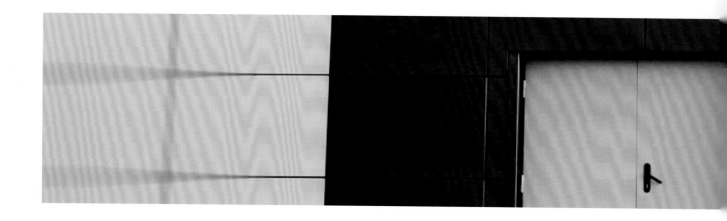

COLIN ELLARD

Colin Ellard is a professor of psychology at the University of Waterloo in Canada, specializing in cognitive neuroscience. He is interested in understanding the emotional effects of architectural settings, which he explores in both field settings and in synthetic environments using immersive virtual reality. Ellard's current projects include exploration of the contribution of peripheral vision to architectural atmosphere, architectural contributions to the emotion of awe, and physiological stress in high-density urban environments. Ellard received his BSc in psychology and philosophy at the University of Toronto and his doctorate at Western University. His latest book is *Places of the Heart: The Psychogeography of Everyday Life* (2015).

➕ COGNITIVE NEUROSCIENCE, URBAN DESIGN, PSYCHOLOGY

Previous: "Astrocyte" (2017) by Philip Beesley/ Living Architecture Systems Group.

As a part of Philip Beesley's Living Architecture Systems Group, my laboratory at the University of Waterloo has been trying to design things that are alive. By that I don't mean that we are mashing up cocktails of organic molecules in the hope that some self-replicating DNA-like substance will emerge. We're doing something that is both simpler and more complicated. The "things" that we design are composed of waving plastic fronds connected to one another with resistance wire, sensors, and distributed networks of simple microprocessors. It's hard to imagine a duller description of what we're doing than this. The magic happens when you see one of these installations in action. Leaflets wave, reach out, recoil, and even sometimes vocalize in response to the movements of interacting humans. When Beesley has set up small-scale versions of these installations for art exhibitions, people will line up for hours for a brief chance to visit. Galleries, institutional buildings, universities, and other interest groups are so clamoring for Beesley's creations that he and his studio can barely keep up with demand. As a psychologist, it's this intense human desire to be near these uncanny creations that fascinates me.

When Philip and I have discussed the installations, we flirt with the word "life." "Near-living" seems like a cowardly retreat. We want to say that the installations are alive. But are they? Here, the struggle becomes real. How do we decide whether something that is patently non-biological is truly alive? As the world's flirtations with novel biomimetic materials and deep learning intensify, I suspect that this is a problem that many of us on this planet will increasingly have to struggle with. A biologist might cite the boilerplate list of criteria for life that we learn about in school – metabolism, self-replication, responsiveness to the environment (or what, curiously, I learned in school to call "irritability"). As a psychologist, though, my answer to that big question feels like a genuflection to Alan Turing and his famous test. Perhaps something is alive when we *feel* as though it is. Admittedly, that definition is not very restrictive. Who among us has not seen life where it makes

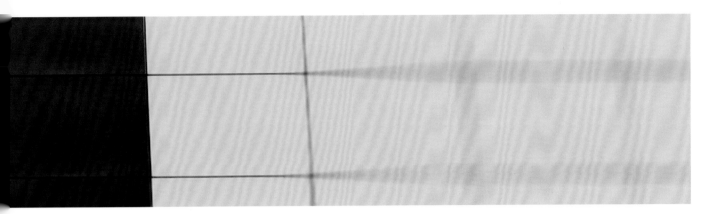

no sense to imagine that it's real? Landmark experiments in psychology by Fritz Heider showed long ago that we even imbue moving colored dots on a screen with complicated lives teeming with aggression, jealousy, love, and fear.[1] When I was a child, I amused myself on long car trips with my parents by imagining that the windshield wipers were alive and chasing one another in a tireless frolic across the rainy glass. Human beings are prone to pareidolic illusions, seeing faces in objects with ease. But though these kinds of definitions of life seem too permissive, there's something compelling about the idea that we recognize life with our hearts as much as with our minds. When we care about something, but especially if we feel that it cares about us, that's when we become the most confident that there's something there – that there's a connection, life, vitality.

When my student Adam Francey and I were trying to brainstorm ways that we might design experiments to ask the right kinds of questions about the roots of our perceptions of life and agency, our thoughts often turned to patterns of visual motion. When gazing into the bed of a stream, how do we see a fish? When watching a tree sway in the wind, how do we notice a hidden squirrel or bird that disturbs the leaves and branches? After some of the most delightful and refreshing field work I've ever done, lying on my back in the grass looking up at trees, we hit upon the idea that the detection of animate life might have to do with a perception of agency – that if something is self-propelled, moved by its own agency, broken out from the camouflage of a sea of movement generated by the currents of wind and water, then we know it's alive. In a way, living things break physics. Based on this proto-idea, we designed some experiments in virtual reality involving balls that fired over a wall towards an observer, following a variety of trajectories. Some followed simple parabolic flights as decreed by Newton, but others were trickier, moving according to an internal logic that we had defined but that was opaque to the observer. These balls were less predictable. They were hard to catch. They were surprising. We hoped that they would look alive.

1 Fritz Heider & Marianne Simmel, An Experimental Study of Apparent Behavior," *The American Journal of Psychology* 57, no. 2 (1944): 243–59.

2 Richard P. Taylor, "Reduction of Physiological Stress Using Fractal Art and Architecture," *Leonardo* 39 (2006): 245–51.

3 Deltcho Valtchanov & Colin Ellard, "Cognitive and Affective Responses to Natural Scenes: Effects of Low-level Visual Properties on Preference, Cognitive Load, and Eye Movements," *Journal of Environmental Psychology* 43 (2015): 184–95.

4 Robert Wurtz, "Recounting the Impact of Hubel and Wiesel," *Journal of Physiology* 587 no. 12 (2009): 2817–23.

5 Irving Biederman & Edward Vessel, "Perceptual Pleasure and the Brain: A Novel Theory Explains Why the Brain Craves Information and Seeks It Through the Senses," *American Scientist* 94, no. 3 (2006): 247–53.

6 Caroline Hagerhall & Rita Berto, "Do Restorative Environments Share Fractal Structural Properties? An Exploratory Research," (paper presented at the International Applied Psychological Society Meeting, Rome, Italy, 2008).

7 Colin Ellard & Charles Montgomery, "Testing, testing! A psychological study on city spaces and how they affect our bodies and minds," (2011) http://cdn.bmwguggenheimlab.org/TESTING_TESTING_BMW_GUGGENHEIM_LAB_2013_2.pdf (accessed August 18, 2018).

8 William H. Whyte, *The Social Life of Small Urban Spaces* (New York: Project for Public Spaces Inc., 1980); Jan Gehl, *Life Between Buildings: Using Public Space* (Washington, DC: Island Press, 2008).

9 Daniel Berlyne, *Conflict, Arousal and Curiosity* (New York: McGraw-Hill, 1960).

10 Arthur E. Stamps, "Entropy, Visual Diversity and Preference," *Journal of General Psychology* 129, no. 3 (2002): 300–20.

11 Samuel Zipp & Nathan Storring (eds), *Vital Little Plans: The Short Works of Jane Jacobs* (Toronto: Random House, 2016), 226.

In another experiment, just now underway, we are using a full-scale installation in Toronto's Royal Ontario Museum to test out some of the same ideas. Here, participants wander through and interact with a room-sized installation. Behind the scenes, we pull subtle strings, manipulating the manner in which the sculpture relates to the behavior of the visitor. Our questions, though, are similar to the ones we ask of participants being pelted with unpredictable virtual balls. Is it alive? Do you care about it? Does it care about you?

In a way, we've been playing with life in my lab for much longer than our involvement in the Living Architecture Systems Group. Some of the first experiments that we conducted in virtual reality were designed to explore the well-known "restorative effect" in environmental psychology. According to what has now become well-trodden dogma, nature refreshes and renews. Though I'm sure human beings have suspected as much for as long as we've been capable of thinking about it, science has found many creative ways to measure this effect. A walk in the woods, a view through a window, or even exposure to an image of nature is said to have beneficial effects on our ability to pay attention, our mood, and even our physiology. Blood pressure and heart rate decrease, stress levels drop, and nervous system arousal levels off. Though these findings are reasonably well documented and have provided the impetus for many design decisions at scales ranging from chemotherapy suites in hospitals to grand urban parks, there has never really been broad agreement on the proximate *causes* of such effects. Some have supposed that the magic might have to do with the specific visual properties of scenes of nature. The physicist Robert Taylor, for example, has argued that scenes of nature possess quite specific fractal properties; that is, natural objects show a kind of self-similarity at a number of scales. Some experiments have purported to show that artificial stimuli that mimic the fractal dimension of scenes of nature are similarly restorative, and may even affect patterns of brain activity.[2] Others, including my group, have suggested that it may not be the fractal dimension per se that tickles the nervous system but

a broader property of visual images called "spatial frequency." In short, low spatial frequencies are the ones that bring us big, blobby contours. High spatial frequencies are found in the fine details in an image. Everyday images contain a broad mixture of spatial frequencies, with some showing through more than others (mathematically speaking, we say that they have more "power"). In experiments in my laboratory conducted by my student Deltcho Valtchanov, we were able to show that the pleasantness and perceived restorativeness of an image could be predicted in part by the spatial frequencies contained in it. Further, whether the image was one of nature or of the built environment, this same general relationship held.[3] We felt that this work lent a nice biological reality to our understanding of the visual properties that produce restoration because the spatial frequency preferences of individual neurons in the visual pathway have been well-documented since David Hubel and Torsten Wiesel's groundbreaking and Nobel-worthy explorations of visual physiology that began in the 1960s.[4]

There's another nice convergence in the work of psychologists Irving Biederman and Edward Vessel, who have shown in imaging experiments that certain higher-tier areas of the visual pathway are particularly interested in the aesthetic properties of scenes, including whether or not they contain elements of nature. Biederman and Vessel have even argued that activation of this part of the brain, which is also rich in opiate receptors, might constitute a part of a reward system in the brain similar to the systems that reinforce us for eating, drinking, or having sex.[5] In this case, though, the reinforcer is exposure to attractive scenes. Biederman's argument, which is in accord with much of the evidence in environmental psychology, is that we may have deeply rooted biological predispositions to be drawn towards scenes of nature because, in our evolutionary beginnings, such predispositions, drawing us perhaps towards natural bounty, would have enhanced our prospects for survival.

As a comprehensive account of the restorative effect, this explanation of mechanism leaves me feeling a little unsatisfied.

Although it might help to explain some aspects of our aesthetic response to scenes of nature (or indeed even certain kinds of urban scenes),[6] it doesn't explain everything. For example, another aspect of the restorative response concerns the manner in which we pay attention to the world. Sometimes called "soft fascination," immersion in a natural scene during the proverbial walk through the woods affords a particular way of paying attention to the world. Our eyes flit from one location to another with little cognitive effort. Contrast this with the situation in a typical urban setting where we often exert strong focal attention on particular elements, sometimes even to preserve our own safety (think of crossing a street). Though one could suppose that in some ill-defined way, the visual patterns in nature encourage us to adopt a different kind of attentional stance to the world, it could also be that natural scenes, because of the types of information they contain and the manner in which that information is distributed throughout a scene, elicit a different kind of paying attention – one that feeds our thirst for novelty, the unexpected, the surprising, the vital, in a way that is not threatening as an oncoming express bus in a busy urban canyon might be.

One of the most satisfying experiences in science is when one discovers that several seemingly unrelated strands of research might share a deep connection. In my own work, another part of my research has focused on field investigations of the impact of street façade design on psychological state. Though this might seem to be a weird kind of niche interest, it began during some work that I conducted for the BMW-Guggenheim Laboratory in 2011 when I designed an experiment that aimed to highlight the impact of urban design variables on our emotional and cognitive state.[7] For one part of the experiment, I had participants stand in front of a long, blank façade in Manhattan while I monitored their psychological state. For contrast, I used another location which had lots of permeability, visual interest, and human action. The results were unequivocal. By every measure that I used, participants standing in front of the blank façade showed physiological and psychological symptoms of abject boredom. Those in front of the lively façade showed a happy, positive state and a healthy nervous system response to stimulation. This result wasn't a complete surprise. In fact, a few minutes spent standing on the street provided strong anecdotal evidence. People hurried past the boring façade with eyes cast downward and attention obviously elsewhere (often on their phone screen) while those walking through the lively area would look around, pause, and show facial expressions that appeared alive and happy. Others have reported similar effects.[8] What our work added to the story was that we were able to use our tools to peer inside the psyches of individual participants, rather than measuring in aggregate from afar.

In addition to the anecdotal evidence from the street, there's well-grounded theory in experimental psychology that might have predicted what we saw in Manhattan. Classical findings in environmental psychology, beginning with the Canadian psychologist Daniel Berlyne, have long suggested that, across a wide range of domains, human beings are attracted to complexity.[9] Indeed, Berlyne was able to show that a variety of different types of animals (in his research mostly laboratory rats) also show a preference for complexity. Though there is far from universal agreement, Berlyne argued for an inverted U-shaped function relating complexity and aesthetic preference, with our strongest preferences being for intermediate levels of complexity. We may not love the overwhelming sensory chaos of a Shibuya Crossing, but neither do we want the long, boring street façades presented by a block-long institutional building like a bank.

As much fun as it is to work in the field—where experiments can be disrupted by sudden rainstorms, road accidents, visits from gregarious drunks, and other sources of experimental error— we decided to further pursue the relationship between façade design and human preference in laboratory experiments using either pictorial displays or immersive virtual reality. Here, we thought, we might have better luck drilling down to the essential elements of aesthetically pleasing façades, so we

felt it worth sacrificing some ecological validity for some scientific rigor. The first task for my student Vedran Dzebic and I to solve was to understand how to quantify complexity. Though not completely satisfying to us, and not comprehensive in its explanatory power, Vedran and I settled on a measure that had been used by some others in the field: "entropy."[10] Without delving too far into the mathematics of the measure, suffice it to say that the measure of entropy we landed on was essentially a description of how much information was present in a scene, using a simple count of the number of different kinds of elements that the scene contained. The higher that number, the higher the entropy of the scene and, we hoped, the more complex, interesting, and attractive it would be judged by an observer. To some extent, we found support for the classic view on the attraction of complexity, but the story was much more nuanced than we had expected it to be.

For one thing, we found that there was a marked difference between viewers' appraisals of the "interest" of a display and its "pleasantness." On the other hand, the relationship between interest and complexity was more straightforward. Generally, we found that our participants judged more complex displays to be more interesting but not necessarily more pleasant. In some cases, participants found very simple displays to be attractive, especially if they contained strong symmetry. Overall, though, without muddying the waters too much with the particularities of our experiments, it's still accurate to say that one of the key drivers of our aesthetic responses to designs, whether they were presented on small computer monitors or at urban scale in the form of streetscapes, had to do with the information that they contained.

Here, we begin to see interesting connections between our separate research projects. What attracts us to nature may be its visual distinctiveness, and especially the manner in which our attention flits without effort from one place to another, each element capturing our interest momentarily with surprise and delight. Just as nature may satisfy our cravings for information, streetscape design containing commodious amounts of activity, opening, and interest will also engage our emotions. We are drawn to life.

As a scientist with strong biological roots, I am tantalized by the possibility that there are deep connections between the detection of animism in creative interactive art, the healthful influences of exposure to nature that arise from a vitality engendered by the unexpected, and engaging urban design that elicits positive affect by offering enough information to satisfy the cravings of our minds. But, at least within the realm of design, I think we can go even further. It may be true that our brains are tuned for novelty wherever they can find it, but it's also obviously true that our response to a setting is influenced by what we understand of its history, its culture, its broader context. I've seen good examples of this in my own work where, for example, participants in my psychogeographic walks are differentially influenced by what they see depending on what they know. In a study we conducted in Germany, we found that many Berliners respond positively to so-called "squatter houses" covered with provocative graffiti and marks of dereliction, whereas tourists might view such settings with anxiety. In one of our other studies, many natives of New York's Lower East Side responded with affection to rows of cinder-block apartments that constituted a part of an affordable housing complex. In this case, at least according to anecdotal accounts given by participants, the positive responses came not from elements of design but from the history of the neighborhood, the people who lived there, the families who played in the small, basic playground that was attached to the building.

These are obvious site-specific examples of the influence of culture and history on response to place. Though we haven't gone looking for them in any systematic way, I'm sure one could find good examples of the influence of such variables in any major city. What interests me more is whether someone experiencing a city neighborhood might be responding

positively to a streetscape for reasons that relate only tangentially, if at all, to our biological heritage but that transcend the particularity of specific cultural or historic references. As often seems to be the case, noted urbanist Jane Jacobs seems to have explored this territory long before me. In a speech given to an urban renewal conference in Hamburg in 1981, Jacobs delivered one of her hallmark diatribes in opposition to what she called "big planning." "Diversity," she says, "is a small-scale phenomenon. It requires collections of little plans."[11] What Jacobs means by diversity in this context is virtually identical to what I have called here complexity. The root of her argument is that city planning, *big* city planning, imposed from the top down, inevitably generates sterile, monolithic boring designs. What I find so interesting about this idea is the suggestion that visual diversity in urban settings might not only arise from a rich, organic, largely unplanned nexus of small plans but that it might also *mark* the process by which such a neighborhood has arisen. We might love the residential neighborhood where every building is distinct not just because of our biological predilection for informational complexity but also because of our affection for the process by which that neighborhood must have come about – the cooperative activity of many people working together to make something emerge that, though it might not be a perfect, gleaming machine, conveys a story about its origin and its evolution.

When I set out, many years ago, to try to understand the human response to the built environment using the tools of experimental psychology, like one of Jane Jacobs's "little planners," I had little in the way of a top-down overarching notion of what it was that I wanted to understand. Instead, I set out to study interesting problems, guided by my nose and also by the passions of the great students I attracted along the way. Looking back on this work now, from what I hope is closer to the midpoint of the journey than its end, I see that, remarkably, much of the work that has been conducted in my lab coalesces around the single, organic, loosely defined idea that we humans seem exquisitely primed to seek out life whether we are wandering a forest,

strolling down a city street, or even exploring a bizarre human-made artistic creation. This thirst for vitality draws our eyes, guides our movements, motivates our thoughts, and even helps to define the urban forms with which we surround ourselves.

SHEIKH-DOWN

Julian Bolleter is an assistant professor at the Australian Urban Design Research Centre at the University of Western Australia where he teaches in the master's program in urban design. He holds a PhD from the University of Western Australia and has worked as a landscape architect in the US, UK, Australia, and Dubai. Bolleter is author or co-author of four books including *Made in Australia: The Future of Australian Cities* (2013, with Richard Weller) and *The Ghost Cities of Australia* (2018).

✛ URBAN DESIGN, LANDSCAPE ARCHITECTURE

Richard Sennett divides the city into two, like a body and a soul. This duality is a comparison between the city as built form and the vitality of urban life that the city form cradles.[1] Landscape architecture has been typically preoccupied with the form (and more recently, ecology) of urban spaces and less concerned about the urban vitality such spaces support. This lack of attention to the social vitality of public spaces has enabled the emergence of a new practice of "placemaking," an unaccredited group of professionals and academics offering an ideology, a theoretical framework, and a set of tools[2] guaranteed to ensure newly designed or retrofitted urban spaces will pull crowds. The origins of the movement derive from 1960s redeemers of dead space like Jane Jacobs and William Whyte who led a revolt against Modernism's abstract and sometimes desolate urban spaces.

Legitimate community expectations and economic motivations drove this shift towards a focus on the lived experience of places and the vitality they generated. At its most aspirational, placemaking "aims to improve the lives of its community"

JULIAN BOLLETER

PLACEMAKING IN DUBAI

through generating urban spaces with sensory richness, attachment, and a deeper meaning based in heritage, character, inclusiveness, and community.[3] The placemaking discipline typically sets out to achieve these aspirations through the programming or "activation" of space. The value of programming urban spaces is now so widely accepted that site activation is synonymous with landscape design and contemporary urban spaces are obliged to look continuously useful.[4]

While I do not consider making the fullest use of urban spaces a bad outcome, this article explores issues that are encountered when placemaking's narrative of equality of access is translated wholesale from the western, democratic contexts from which the placemaking movement emerged, to "foreign" contexts such as Dubai, which are autocratic

and socio-culturally highly segregated environments. I argue that in such contexts placemaking often (though not always) collapses into a form of place branding that commodifies places, obscures societal segregation, serves dictatorial political agendas,[5] diminishes urban authenticity, restricts alternative ways of using spaces, and (in some respects) hinders the organic formation of a less artificially constructed society.

This shift to place branding is not just occurring in Dubai. The Project for Public Spaces—which coined the term placemaking— has identified that many planners and developers now use placemaking as a "brand to imply authenticity and quality, even if their projects don't always live up to that promise."[6] The issue with the rise of place branding is that by scripting the identity of urban development, place branding threatens cultural, social, and experiential diversity, as Nicole Porter explains, "by offering the public...no choice but to be consumers; every landscape we engage with will be the product of the same system and logic."[7]

Dubai is host to a particularly pronounced shift from placemaking to place branding because as a Florian Kaefer (editor of *The Place Brand Observer* website) explains, "Dubai's ability to set long-term visions and plan accordingly without much interference of opposing opinions is a place brander's dream."[8] Moreover, Dubai is heavily reliant on placemaking to develop constructed attractions and experiences to lure global capital, wealthy tourists, and "the creative class" who are seen to spur economic development.

Landscape architects should be aware of this situation because in Dubai, and elsewhere, placemaking (hereafter including the related practice of place branding) now frames the design brief and project rationale that landscape architects must respond to, and as such placemaking, indirectly or otherwise, dictates the landscape architectural outcomes themselves.[9] Indeed as Ismail Hammadi elaborates, new projects in Dubai–such as Dubai Design District, Dubai Canal, and Dubai South–have been created and designed with the *sole purpose* of placemaking.[10] As such, a critical appraisal of placemaking is timely. But my argument here is not with placemaking professionals themselves; it is with the ways in which placemaking (and the other urban professions) has been coopted by developers and marketers, as a brand for major urban projects in Dubai and elsewhere.

Placemaking Dubai

Dubai in the first decade of this century was known for its engineering feats, architectural gymnastics, and shopping malls; however, it is increasingly becoming recognized for its large-scale events and festivals. As a result, its proponents now perceive Dubai as the foremost city in the region for the creative industries, with increased "brand recognition" in this respect. Facilitating this shift has been an approach to urban development that puts the visitor's experience at its core, with placemaking playing a key role. As Hadley Newman describes, visitors to Dubai "are seeking an experience, they want to take it home with them, or look back on an event as something like a new adventure – one that they may never have a chance to do again. People expect a complete experience that is distinctive in each place."[11]

While advocates for placemaking in the Western world articulate it as a bottom-up process, in Dubai, unelected ruler Sheikh Mohammed bin Rashid al Maktoum has driven the placemaking component of key urban projects. In a bid to turn Dubai into one of the cultural epicenters of the world, he urged in 2014, "Let us work as one team to transform our city into a cultural hub that attracts creative artists...a vibrant place for all."[12] Supporting these ambitions is a government-set target of 20 million tourists visiting the city annually by 2020.

Delivering this cultural experience are Dubai's gargantuan property developers including Emaar, Meraas, Dubai Properties, and Nakheel – all of which are linked to Sheikh Mohammed and his ruling family, and have placemaking-driven urban projects underway around the city. Moreover, "Brand Dubai," the creative arm of the Government of Dubai Media Office, supports these developers, through street art and art installations that "communicate positive messages about Dubai's unique culture, values and identity,"[13] and by extension, Dubai's leadership.

Most significant of the urban projects is the revitalization and extension of the historic Dubai Creek districts, an area that Sheikh Mohammed describes as the "very heart and soul of Dubai." Other key projects driven by placemaking approaches are the Dubai Design District, which is planned to positively reflect on Dubai's brand through designer fashion and interior design; Jumeriah Beach Walk, which offers up an image of a bustling yet exclusive coastal promenade; and City Walk, which showcases Dubai's emerging (yet largely faux) urbanity. While collectively these projects are elegantly designed and enjoyable to visit, this article interrogates the socio-cultural agendas which these projects embody, a dimension of such projects which the urban professions (inclusive of placemaking) tend to overlook.

Sanitizing Urban Life

One of the key values of urban public space is that it carries the potential for random social encounters. Richard Sennet argues that such encounters with difference is the key quality of true urbanity – that the density and diversity of people in public space has a civilizing function that produces tolerance of difference, and enables the formation of new identities.[14] Sennett refers to this ideal as "the open city" in that it frees people from the straitjacket of the "fixed and the familiar, creating a terrain in which they could experiment and expand their experience."[15]

Clearly, a very multicultural city such as Dubai *could* function as Sennett suggests; however, this is (often) not the case. Instead, placemaking in Dubai carefully packages urban projects to offer highly choreographed and exclusive experiences for wealthy consumers, whether tourists or locals. Dubai's unskilled migrant underclass is effectively denied entry to such heavily place-branded projects – not by fences, but by various "soft" strategies including high parking fees, lack of public transport, and aesthetic codes that signify a project's exclusiveness.[16] The result is that such projects often become "protected playgrounds" that strip away the uncertainty and anonymity from urban life.[17] As Kim Dovey suggests, this "avoidance of risk leads [to the] sanitization" of the urban experience,[18] which otherwise enriches a city's culture. Dovey advocates that in most urban spaces, spatial and programmatic *under*-determination is in fact the better approach, as an overdetermined design and management regime often locks in one "right" way of using a place and precludes other ways of using and occupying a space.[19]

It is well known that creativity flourishes best in a unique social environment. One that is stable enough to allow continuity of effort, yet diverse and broad-minded enough to nourish creativity in all its potentially subversive and non-scripted forms.[20] The issue for Sheikh Mohammed is that, as he strives to transition Dubai into a "cultural hub that attracts creative artists," he needs to allow genuine subversion – subversion which could loosen his hold on power over the longer term.

Eroding Identity

Much of the placemaking delivered in Dubai has been focused on recreating the traditional urban forms of a pre-petroleum Dubai, as destinations for Emiratis and wealthy tourists and expatriates. Examples of this nostalgia-laced placemaking include the Old Town, Souq Al Bahar, and Souq Madinat Jumeirah, as well as the revitalization of Dubai's historic Creek districts.

The placemakers who conducted a placemaking study of the Creek districts described their excitement at "uncovering plans of the earlier town layout" that revealed the "historic tradition of passive solar design at the urban scale, wind management and its exploitation as a cooling device...a great story for the marketing team."[21] The indirect result of such studies has been projects such as Al Seef and Culture Village (both farther up Dubai Creek), which have imitated the vernacular urban forms of the region to varying degrees of accuracy. While popular with tourists, it is worth noting that, as Koolhaas has warned:

> History has an invidious half-life – as it is more abused, it becomes less significant, to the point where its diminishing handouts become more insulting. This thinning is exacerbated by the constantly increasing mass of tourists, an avalanche that, in a perpetual quest for "character," grinds successful identities into dust.[22]

This is certainly the case with Culture Village. While its marketing proclaims that "with its own cultural and exhibition centers and signature residences and shopping complexes, the development is a tribute to the cultural diversity of Dubai," the development is in fact a bounded place to be experienced and consumed by the wealthy. Moreover, its proponents claim, "Culture Village seeks to rejuvenate the romance and mystique of a civilization that flourished by the creek, providing the canvas for vibrant living and play."[23] The problem with this deceptively romantic take on a hard-working port that has been a haven and haunt of smugglers and pirates over thousands of years is that the project confuses and strips away the authenticity of the area. As Naomi Klein has argued, "The terrible irony of these surrogates, of course, is how destructive they are to the real thing."[24]

Legitimizing Ruling Elites

Further to its superficiality, the placemaking (and design) profession's willingness to revive such traditional charades has a political dimension that goes unacknowledged. Cities do not "have" a memory – they "make" one for themselves with the aid of symbols, images, rites, ceremonies, places, and monuments.[25] In this respect Dubai's rulers use nostalgic urban forms, generated through placemaking, to construct a narrative that

1 Justin McGuirk, "Can Cities Make Us Better Citizens?," *The New Yorker*, https://www.newyorker.com/books/page-turner/can-cities-make-us-better-citizens.

2 Ruth Fincher, Maree Pardy & Kate Shaw, "Place-Making or Place-Masking? The Everyday Political Economy of "Making Place," *Planning Theory & Practice* 17, no. 4 (2016): 519.

3 Ibid., 518.

4 Karl Kullmann, "The Usefulness of Uselessness: Towards a Landscape Framework for Un-Activated Urban Public Space," *Architectural Theory Review* 19, no. 2 (2014): 155.

5 Krista Paulsen, "Placemaking," in *Encyclopedia of Urban Studies* (Sage, 2010), 2.

6 Project for Public Spaces, "What Is Placemaking?" https://www.pps.org/article/what-is-placemaking.

7 Nicole Porter, "Branding Landscape," *LA+ Interdisciplinary Journal of Landscape Architecture*, no. 5 (2017): 89.

8 Florian Kaefer, "Dubai, a Place Brander's Dream," *Gulf Marketing Review*, https://gulfmarketingreview.com/opinion/dubai-place-branders-dream/.

9 Porter, "Branding Landscape," 88.

10 Ismail Al Hammadi, "Placemaking and Destination Branding - How It Changed Dubai's Architecture for the Past 10 Years," https://www.linkedin.com/pulse/placemaking-destination-branding-how-...1.

11 Hadley Newman, "How Creative Placemaking Is Helping Put Dubai on the Cultural Map," http://inbusiness.ae/2016/07/20/how-creative-placemaking-is-helping-put-dubai-on-the-cultural-map/.

12 Aarti Nagraj, "Dubai's Ruler Approves Dhs2bn Creek Front Project," Gulf Business, http://gulfbusiness.com/dubais-ruler-approves-dhs2bn-creek-front-project/.

13 Brand Dubai, "Brand Dubai," http://www.branddubai.com/indexen.php/.

14 Kim Dovey, *Fluid City: Transforming Melbourne's Urban Waterfront* (London: Routledge, 2005), 16.

15 McGuirk, "Can Cities Make Us Better Citizens?"

16 Dovey, *Fluid City*, 15. Moreover, social divisions in Dubai are created by seduction and desire rather than regulation and coercion – oppression in Dubai comes with glossy brochures and red-carpeted entrances: Michele Acuto, "High-Rise Dubai Urban Entrepreneurialism and the Technology of Symbolic Power," *Cities* 27 (2010): 281.

17 Kim Dovey, *Urban Design Thinking* (London: Bloomsbury Academic, 2016), 48.

Previous: An uninhabited yet heavily place-managed urban space in Dubai Design District.

the authority of Sheikh Mohammed sits in a "natural line of progress"[26] extending from Dubai's ancient history to the current day. The propagation of such narratives in Dubai is a flow-on effect of the Arab Spring, which has seen a harsher tone on issues of identity and national culture, with increasingly open calls by locals for state intervention to defend against "threats" allegedly posed by foreigners to "national culture."[27]

One of the reasons the Arab Spring has not undermined the ruling elites in Dubai (and the UAE more generally) is that the rulers have been able to maintain the "social contract" with the populace which ensures that they have not faced a crisis of legitimacy.[28] This social contract involves the provision of jobs and housing but also highly symbolic urban projects such as those along Dubai Creek that in part seek to "naturalize" the rule of the unelected leader. The fact that Sheikh Mohammed has taken such a keen interest in branding urban open spaces in Dubai is not coincidental – the mobilizations of the Arab Spring all took place in urban spaces such as Tahir Square in Cairo and Bahrain's Pearl Roundabout. Sheikh Mohammed's attempts to promote particular nostalgic images of urban spaces in Dubai are, in part, an attempt to claim these spaces as not being open to appropriation for protests – subtle or overt. Lacing placemaking in Dubai is complex power relations, all of which remain under-theorized and unacknowledged in much of the placemaking literature.[29]

Significance

This article has made the case that placemaking in Dubai (in many instances) has collapsed into a form of place branding that obscures societal exclusion, serves autocratic political agendas, and grinds down urban authenticity. This recalls Jane Jacobs's famous remark, "There is a quality even meaner than outright ugliness or disorder, and this meaner quality is the dishonest mask of pretended order, achieved by ignoring or suppressing the real order that is struggling to exist and to be served." [30]

Generally, the inclusive language of placemaking masks a process of urban development in Dubai that has negligible benefits for Dubai's substantial underclass who embody the real order to which Jacobs refers. There are understandable reasons for why this has happened – not least of which is that placemaking is a service industry that depends on clients who have no interest in expressing this "real order" in their exclusive urban developments. However, as Dubai's development companies are exporting their models of development to a vast region (including China, India, Africa, Jordan, Tunisia, Morocco, Turkey, Egypt, Brazil, and Baku), it is important that placemaking's role in this culturally impoverishing model of development is subjected to scrutiny.

18 Dovey, *Fluid City*, 15.

19 Dovey, *Urban Design Thinking*, 42.

20 Richard Florida, *Rise of the Creative Class* (New York: Basic Books, 2002), 35.

21 Kylie Legge, "Cultural Glue: The Secret to Making Great Places," *Ar Public Journal* 2018, no. 105 (2008): 64.

22 O.M.A, Rem Koolhaas & Bruce Mau, *S,M,L,XL* (New York: Monacelli Press, 1995), 1248.

23 Dubai Properties, "Dubai Wharf," Dubai Properties, https://richlanddubai.com/wp-content/uploads/2017/07/Dubai-Wharf-Brochure.pdf.

24 Naomi Klein, *No Logo* (London: Flamingo, 2000), 176.

25 Anita Bakshi, "Urban Form and Memory Discourses: Spatial Practices in Contested Cities," *Journal of Urban Design* 19, no. 2 (2014): 191.

26 Dovey, *Urban Design Thinking*, 128.

27 Ahmed Kanna, "Flexible Citizenship in Dubai: Neoliberal Subjectivity in the Emerging "City Corporation," *Cultural Anthropology* 25, no. 1 (2010): 124.

28 Ingo Forstenlechner, Emilie Rutledge & Rashed Salem Alnuaimi, "The UAE, the Arab Spring and Different Types of Dissent," The Middle East Policy Council.

29 Fincher, Pardy & Shaw, "Place-Making or Place-Masking?" 519.

30 Ibid., 534.

Left: A South Asian migrant worker polishes the faux dusty floor of the reconstructed "heritage" Al Seef development on Dubai Creek.

BILLIE GILES-CORTI, JONATHAN ARUNDEL + LUCY GUNN
DESIGNING HEALTHY, LIVABLE CITIES

Billie Giles-Corti is a distinguished professor at RMIT University in Melbourne, Australia, and director of its Urban Futures Enabling Capability Platform. She is a National Health and Medical Research Council Senior Principal Research Fellow and directs the Centre for Urban Research's Healthy Liveable Cities Research Group. Giles-Corti is an honorary fellow of both the Planning Institute of Australia and the Public Health Association. She has over 300 publications and by citations is ranked in the top 1% of researchers in her field globally.

Jonathan Arundel is a senior research fellow with the Healthy Liveable Cities Group at RMIT University. He holds a PhD in geomatics from the University of Melbourne and has 15 years' experience in the telecommunications and transportation industries. His background spans agent-based modeling, remote sensing and ecology, and spatial methods including GIS. Arundel is currently leading the development of a national livability indicator geospatial database in Australia.

Lucy Gunn is a research fellow with the Healthy Liveable Cities Group at RMIT University and holds a PhD in econometrics from Monash University. Her research uses quantitative techniques to explore the relationship between the built environment and health and well-being outcomes. Gunn's current research and consultancy projects explore the relationship between policy targets and on-the-ground infrastructure delivery and health.

+ PUBLIC HEALTH, URBAN PLANNING

In Lewis Carroll's enduring tale *Alice's Adventures in Wonderland*, adventurous Alice asks the Cheshire Cat which way she should go from here, to which the Cat quips that it depends on where she wants to get to. As we confront the prospect of nearly 70% of the world's population urbanized by 2050, citizens and those who design, build, manage, and govern cities might ask themselves the same question: where do we want to get to?

Some sectors might approach this question in a values-free way, but the health sector has a clear vision for cities, based on recognition of an urgent need to create health-promoting conditions for urban dwellers. The burden of preventable chronic disease is crippling health systems globally, prompting the United Nations (UN) to call for multisector, whole-of-society action to curb and prevent these diseases.[1] Although it is the health sector that treats disease, other sectors can help prevent disease by determining whether "healthy choices are easy choices."[2] Hence, for decades, the World Health Organization (WHO) has championed the creation of "healthy cities" that foster healthy lifestyles and equity.[3] WHO's position was reaffirmed in its 2016 Shanghai Declaration, which stated that cities are "critical settings for health," and that health is one of the "most effective markers of sustainable development."[4] This declaration followed two earlier landmark WHO reports: the report by the Social Determinants of Health Commission,[5] which concluded that health and health equity should be at the heart of city governance, and the Hidden Cities report, published jointly with UN Habitat,[6] which highlighted an urgent need to identify and remove health inequities. From a health sector perspective, cities that encourage physically and socially active lifestyles and provide equitable access to the amenities and services required for daily living will support health by creating supportive environments that promote healthy, sustainable lifestyles.[7]

This article briefly reviews the evidence on why the design of cities is so important for the health and well-being of their residents. It introduces the concept of livability–defined in health terms–and considers the policies required to create healthy, livable cities. In the Australian context, it draws on recent research to consider whether we have the policy and implementation frameworks in place to create healthy, livable cities. Finally, it considers consumer demand: are urban dwellers getting what they want, or is there a latent demand for more walkable cities?

Why Urban Design is Important

Globally, the prevalence of non-communicable diseases is increasing, accounting for more than 66% of all deaths annually.[8] The most common non-communicable diseases (cardiovascular disease, diabetes, and some cancers) share risk factors that are influenced by the way cities are designed, planned, and governed. For example, low-density housing on the urban fringe, poorly served by public transit, increases residents' dependency on motor vehicles. This in turn reduces physical activity, leads to sedentariness and obesity, and increases air pollution – all major risk factors for non-communicable diseases. The economic burden of these preventable diseases is a heavy one for health systems around the world – one that it cannot tackle alone. Indeed, there is growing recognition of the need for integrated, whole-of-government, whole-of-society action to combat non-communicable diseases[9] and reduce health inequity[10] (that is, avoidable inequalities in health).[11] Such action includes creating cities that encourage physically and socially active lifestyles by designing walkable communities with better access to public transport, shops, services, and public open space. Cities with these amenities will reduce the risk of obesity and help create more socially equitable and inclusive communities.[12]

The need for urban planning and design to accommodate public health concerns is now recognized globally. For example, the United Nations has called for multisector action—including by the professions that build cities—to curb non-communicable disease.[13] The UN Sustainable Development Goals focus on reducing poverty and inequality, and therefore include goals and targets for creating more sustainable, inclusive cities and promoting health and well-being for all.[14] Recent OECD reports also call for multisector leadership from "transport, land use, and health ministers" to establish the technical, legislative, and regulatory frameworks that encourage walking;[15] and for city planning that improves air quality, because of its substantial effect on people's health.[16] Collectively, these reports signal high-level agreement on the need for integrated, multisector planning and action, and recognize that support for public health should be a central consideration in city planning.

These ideas are not new: during 19th-century industrialization, city authorities attempted to tackle poverty, overcrowding, industrial pollution, and communicable and waterborne diseases, in order to improve public health and reduce health inequities.[17] But in the 21st century, the major threats to health faced by city dwellers—including in developing countries—are preventable chronic diseases, which have been partly caused by well-intentioned efforts to protect the public from infectious disease and to improve quality of life: that is, by separating land uses, promoting low-density suburban sprawl, and designing cities to make it easier to travel by private motor vehicles.

Creating Healthy, Livable Cities

Efforts to promote health and reduce non-communicable diseases and health inequity complement city planning and global efforts to create more sustainable and resilient cities. Cities already generate 70% of global greenhouse gas emissions.[18] If we continue with business as usual, these emissions will undoubtedly rise as urban populations grow. Poor air quality and high levels of particulates and other emissions directly harm human respiratory health and contribute to cardiovascular disease.[19] Greenhouse gas emissions contribute to climate change, which leads to more frequent extreme weather events that damage people's physical and mental health and can lead to infectious diseases and heat stress. Climate change also depletes essential resources such as food and water. For all these reasons, climate change and its causes are now recognized as a threat to, but also an opportunity to improve, public health.[20] Indeed, making the transition to more environmentally friendly cities that foster more sustainable active lifestyles will reduce the prevalence of non-communicable diseases,[21] while also mitigating the threats posed by climate change. One path to creating sustainable, resilient cities that promote health is to design cities that are compact, pedestrian- and cycling-friendly, less dependent on automobiles, and more socially inclusive.[22] These cities will also be more livable. Moreover, in keeping with the theme of this issue, a livable city has vitality and, in turn, fosters the vitality of its residents.

The concept of livability resonates with local, state, federal, and global decision-makers, and with the wider community. Yet, although it often features in public and policy discourse, it is rarely defined. Based on a comprehensive review of the literature in 2013, our team defined livable cities that promote health and well-being as those that are safe and socially cohesive and inclusive; are environmentally sustainable; and offer affordable and diverse housing linked by public transport, walking and cycling infrastructure to employment, public open space, and all the amenities and services needed for daily living.[23]

1 United Nations (UN) General Assembly, *Political Declaration of the High-Level Meeting of the General Assembly on the Prevention and Control of Non-Communicable Diseases* (New York: United Nations, 2011).

2 World Health Organization (WHO), "The Ottawa Charter for Health Promotion," *Health Promotion International* 1 (1986): 3–5.

3 Evelyne de Leeuw, "Healthy Cities Deserve Better," *Lancet* 380, no. 9850 (2012): 1306–07.

4 WHO, "Shanghai Declaration on Promoting Health in the 2030 Agenda for Sustainable Development" (paper presented at the WHO 9th Global Conference on Health Promotion, Shanghai, 2016).

5 WHO Commission on the Social Determinants of Health, *Closing the Gap in a Generation: Health Equity through Action on the Social Determinants of Health. Final Report of the Commission on the Social Determinants of Health* (Geneva: World Health Organization, 2008).

6 WHO & UN Habitat, *Hidden Cities: Unmasking and Overcoming Health Inequities in Urban Settings* (Geneva: World Health Organization, 2010).

7 Billie Giles-Corti, et al., "City Planning and Population Health: A Global Challenge," *Lancet* 388, no. 10062 (2016): 2912–24.

8 Rafael Lozano, et al., "Global and Regional Mortality from 235 Causes of Death for 20 Age Groups in 1990 and 2010: A Systematic Analysis for the Global Burden of Disease Study 2010," *Lancet* 380, no. 9859 (2012): 2095–128.

9 Stephen S. Lim, et al., "A Comparative Risk Assessment of Burden of Disease and Injury Attributable to 67 Risk Factors and Risk Factor Clusters in 21 Regions, 1990–2010: A Systematic Analysis for the Global Burden of Disease Study 2010," *Lancet* 380, no. 9859 (2012): 2224–60; Pedro C. Hallal, et al., "Global Physical Activity Levels: Surveillance Progress, Pitfalls, and Prospects," *Lancet* 380, no. 9838 (2012): 247–57.

The foundations of a livable city are higher-density walkable neighborhoods,[24] with connected street networks that facilitate convenient and safe access to local shops, community and recreational services, and employment, using active and sustainable modes of transport: walking, cycling, and public transit. While local urban design is essential for creating walkable neighborhoods, alone it is insufficient to maximize local walking. Building on the work of transport and urban planners Ewing and Cervero,[25] we have argued for the need for eight interventions: three regional planning interventions (destination accessibility, distribution of employment, and demand management (e.g., the amount and cost of car parking)); and five local urban design interventions (design, density, distance to transit, diversity (of housing and mixed uses), and desirability (personal and traffic safety, and conviviality)).[26] Although these interventions will be delivered in different ways in different contexts, they are all important, as they work together to create healthy, livable cities that foster local walking. Hence, integrated planning is needed across urban systems including land use, transport, and social infrastructure policies (education, health and social, cultural); as well as public open space, housing, building design, and public safety.[27] Importantly, integrated policies that help build healthy, equitable, livable cities would not only promote health, but would also create more sustainable and inclusive cities, and help achieve many of the UN Sustainable Development Goals.

Are We on Track?

Despite the rhetoric and urgency of the need for healthier, more sustainable cities, do we have policies that help create such places? And if we do, are those policies actually being implemented? These were the questions behind a recent nationwide Australian study, which examined the city planning policies for seven "domains" of livability known to encourage better health: walkability, public open space, public transport, employment, affordable housing, healthy food choices, and fewer alcohol outlets.[28] The research involved a policy review to identify spatial standards and targets designed to create healthy, livable cities, and spatial mapping of those policies to identify in which part of the city these policies were being fully implemented.

We found inconsistent standards and targets between Australia's state government jurisdictions, differing levels of policy ambition as reflected in policy targets, and significant variation in the implementation of standards and targets in cities. For example, at the time of the review, dwelling density (the cornerstone of healthy, livable, walkable neighborhoods)[29] was set at 26 dwellings per hectare in Western Australia and 15 dwellings per hectare in Victoria and New South Wales, while in Queensland the target was 30 dwellings per hectare in urban areas, and 15 for suburban development.[30] Densities of 15 dwellings per hectare are generally too low to achieve walkable neighborhoods. Recent Australian research shows that to encourage walking, cycling, and public transport use—and discourage driving—densities of at least 25 to 30 dwellings per hectare are required.[31] This is because higher-density neighborhoods create a local economy that supports more local destinations and transit: if residents are to walk locally, they need destinations to walk to.[32] Yet, with the exception of Sydney (Australia's most populous city), there was little evidence of even these modest policy targets being met in Australia. However, to encourage local walking, density must be complemented by other local features: diverse housing, connected street networks that offer easy access to public transit and local destinations, and urban and building design and landscape architecture that create a safer and more desirable neighborhood.[33]

Similarly, although access to public open space is crucial, the study of Australia's major cities found no agreed standards for proximity, type, or size of public open space. Although some states had standards for proximity (for instance, within 400 meters) for different types of parks (such as a neighborhood, district, or regional parks), or specified sizes, other states had no such requirements. As a consequence,

10 Michael Marmot, *Fair Society, Healthy Lives: The Marmot Review: Strategic Review of Health Inequalities in England Post-2010* (London: UCL Institute for Health Equity, 2011).

11 WHO Commission on the Social Determinants of Health, *Closing the Gap in a Generation*.

12 UN General Assembly, *Political Declaration...On the Prevention and Control of Non-Communicable Diseases*.

13 Ibid.

14 UN General Assembly, *Transforming Our World: The 2030 Agenda for Sustainable Development* (New York: United Nations, 2015).

15 Organisation for Economic Co-operation and Development (OECD), *International Transport Forum 2011: Pedestrian Survey: Urban Space and Health: Summary Document* (OECD Publishing, 2011).

16 OECD, *The Cost of Air Pollution: Health Impacts of Road Transport* (Paris: OECD Publishing, 2014).

17 Jason Corburn, "Reconnecting with Our Roots: American Urban Planning and Public Health in the Twenty-First Century," *Urban Affairs Review* 42, no. 5 (2007): 688–713.

18 WHO & UN Habitat, *Global Report on Urban Health: Equitable Healthier Cities for Sustainable Development* (Italy: WHO, 2016).

19 Giles-Corti, et al., "City Planning and Population Health."

20 Andy Haines, et al., "Public Health Benefits of Strategies to Reduce Greenhouse-Gas Emissions: Overview and Implications for Policy Makers," *Lancet* 374, no. 9707 (2009): 2104–14; Nick Watts, et al., "Health and Climate Change: Policy Responses to Protect Public Health," *Lancet* 386, no. 10006 (2015): 1861–914.

21 Watts, et al., "Health and Climate Change."

in Victoria for example, we found no association between recreational walking or mental health with access to parks within 400 meters – an outcome, we found, was due to an over-reliance on creating parks of less than one hectare.[34] Moreover, none of the policies reviewed considered public open space requirements in higher-density areas. As cities densify and become more compact to achieve a more sustainable future, greater consideration will need to be given to the amounts of public open space required as residents lose access to private open space.

The study also identified significant spatial inequalities in the implementation of policy standards designed to create healthy, livable communities. Almost without exception, compared with residents of outer and middle-level suburbs, urban (central city) residents were substantially better served by the integrated planning needed for walkable urban design and local amenities, public transit, and infrastructure. A notable absence was well-implemented integrated policy aimed at creating walkable outer-suburban development, despite these areas having better access to public open space. This lack is exacerbating health, economic, and environmental inequities, fueled by motor vehicle dependency, traffic congestion, vehicle kilometers traveled, and greenhouse gas emissions, as well as heat island effects caused by the proliferation of carparks and roads. By not placing a value on health and livability, we will continue to design our cities around private motor vehicles, to the detriment of residents' well-being. Finally, we found that although the concept of livability and walkable communities appears in policy discourse, Australian cities appear to lack the policies necessary to achieve these aspirations.

Do People Want More Walkable Communities?

The continued proliferation of urban sprawl on the fringes of cities is often said to reflect market preferences, with developers hesitant to change their building practices. But the main factor determining people's choice of housing is affordability,[35] with safe, pedestrian-friendly neighborhoods a strong secondary preference. Indeed, an Australian Heart Foundation consumer survey found that, when deciding where

22 Major Cities Unit, *State of Australian Cities, 2010* (Canberra: Major Cities Unit, Infrastructure Australia, 2010); Department of Infrastructure and Transport, *Our Cities, Our Future: A National Urban Policy for a Productive, Sustainable and Liveable Future* (Canberra: Department of Infrastructure and Transport, 2011); Western Australian Planning Commission, *Liveable Neighbourhoods: A Western Australian Government Sustainable Cities Initiative* (Perth: Western Australian Planning Commission, 2007).

23 Hannah Badland, et al., "Urban Liveability: Emerging Lessons from Australia for Exploring the Potential for Indicators to Measure the Social Determinants of Health," *Social Science & Medicine* 111C (2014): 64–73; Melanie Lowe, et al., *Liveable, Healthy, Sustainable: What Are the Key Indicators for Melbourne Neighbourhoods?* (Melbourne: University of Melbourne, 2013).

24 Paula Hooper, et al., "The Building Blocks of a 'Liveable Neighbourhood': Identifying the Key Performance Indicators for Walking of an Operational Planning Policy in Perth, Western Australia," *Health Place* 36 (2015): 173–83.

25 Reid Ewing & Robert Cervero, "Travel and the Built Environment: A Meta-Analysis," *Journal of the American Planning Association* 76, no. 3 (2010): 265–94.

26 Giles-Corti, et al., "City Planning and Population Health."

27 Ibid.

28 Jonathan Arundel, et al., *Creating Liveable Cities in Australia: Mapping Urban Policy Implementation and Evidence-Based National Liveability Indicators* (Melbourne: Centre for Urban Research, RMIT University, 2017).

Neighborhood preference by walkability of residents' current neighborhood

Preferred neighborhood type	Actual walkability of current neighborhood*		
	Low-walkable % n=603	High-walkable % n=606	Total % n=1,209
Where shops, restaurants, cafés, libraries, and other services are separate from houses (say 1.5 kilometers or more), even if it means residents cannot walk to these facilities.	40.5	36.6	38.5
No preference	9.5	7.9	8.7
Where residents can walk to shops, restaurants, cafés, libraries, or other services, even if this means that the shops and services are within a few blocks (500 meters) of houses.	50.1	55.4	52.8

*Objectively measured based on dwelling density, street connectivity, and mixed uses.

to live, 70% of people considered access to public transit and 64% considered being within easy walking distance of local services to be either extremely important or very important factors.[36]

Australian studies suggest a preference for walkable neighborhoods among people living in suburban developments. The RESIDE study was a longitudinal evaluation of a state government land subdivision design code, which surveyed the same residents three times after they had relocated to new homes in a new neighborhood, some of which were designed in accordance with the new subdivision design code.[37] As shown in the adjacent table, there was some dissonance between residential location and neighborhood preferences in those living in both low-walkable and high-walkable neighborhoods. However, after living in their new neighborhood for around seven to nine years, 50% of those living in low-walkable neighborhoods said they would prefer to live within walking distance of local shops and services, while only 38.5% overall preferred neighborhoods separated from local shops and services.

These results reveal a potential latent demand for walkable neighborhoods in low-density suburban areas: neighborhoods that are close to shops, services, and public transit. Rather than continuing to build low-density suburban sprawl, developers would have to work differently in outer-suburban areas, providing diverse housing, mixed uses, and medium- to high-density housing, particularly around transport hubs that connect residents to employment centers. Given that walkability often attracts a property value premium, how can we ensure that this type of development remains affordable? The public health gains are self-evident.

What Next?

We have no time to waste in creating cities that are more sustainable and resilient: on our watch, the world's population is growing and urbanizing at an unprecedented rate. One way to achieve this goal is to create healthy, livable cities with the amenities required for daily living, accessible through active transport and transit. Critically–from a public health perspective–healthy, livable cities should be underpinned by walkable neighborhoods, because this will encourage physically and socially active lifestyles, and habitual incidental physical activity. Across whole populations, the health gains of doing so would substantially reduce preventable disease and spatial inequalities.[38]

However, we have a long way to go, particularly in Australia and North America, and multisector partnerships are needed. Indeed, as the OECD argues, it will require "transport, land use, and health ministers" (and also, we would argue, infrastructure ministers) to establish the technical, legislative, regulatory, and financing frameworks to achieve this goal, but also urban planners and designers to plan and design more walkable and sustainable developments, and the private sector to develop new business models.[39]

The health, social, economic, and environmental consequences of the city planning and design choices and decisions we make today will be borne by future generations. Returning to the question of "where do we want to get to?," the clear answer from a public health perspective is healthy, livable, and more sustainable cities, which foster active and sustainable lifestyles that support both individual and planetary health. But the health sector does not build cities: this is the responsibility of urban designers, planners, and other built-environment professionals. If we are to undertake the journey together, we will all want to get to the same destination. There is a growing body of public health evidence on the design of cities that foster health and well-being; the question is, how can the public health community effectively share this knowledge and work with urban designers and others to design, build, and evaluate our cities, with the aim of bringing health and well-being to all?

29 Hooper, et al., "The Building Blocks of a 'Liveable Neighbourhood.'"

30 Arundel, et al., *Creating Liveable Cities in Australia.*

31 Claire Boulange, et al., "Examining Associations between Urban Design Attributes and Transport Mode Choices for Walking, Cycling, Public Transport and Private Motor Vehicle Trips," *Journal of Transport and Health* 6 (2017): 155–66.

32 Hooper, et al., "The Building Blocks of a 'Liveable Neighbourhood.'"

33 Giles-Corti, et al., "City Planning and Population Health."

34 Mohammad Javad Koohsari, et al., "Are Public Open Space Attributes Associated with Walking and Depression?," *Cities* 74 (2018): 119–25.

35 Billie Giles-Corti, et al., "Evaluation of the Implementation of a State Government Community Design Policy Aimed at Increasing Local Walking: Design Issues and Baseline Results from RESIDE, Perth, Western Australia," *Preventive Medicine* 46, no. 1 (2008): 46–54.

36 Heart Foundation of Australia (NSW Division), *Creating Healthy Neighbourhoods: Consumer Preferences for Healthy Development* (Sydney: Heart Foundation of Australia NSW Division, 2011).

37 Giles-Corti, et al., "Evaluation of the Implementation of a State Government Community Design Policy."

38 Mark Stevenson, et al., "Land Use, Transport, and Population Health: Estimating the Health Benefits of Compact Cities," *Lancet* 388, no. 10062 (2016): 2925–35.

39 OECD, *International Transport Forum 2011.*

Acknowledgments: Billie Giles-Corti is supported by an NHMRC Senior Principal Research Fellowship, Jonathan Arundel is supported The Australian Prevention Partnership Centre and Clean Air and Urban Landscapes Hub of the National Environmental Science Programme, and Lucy Gunn is supported by the NHMRC Centre of Research Excellence in Healthy Liveable Communities.

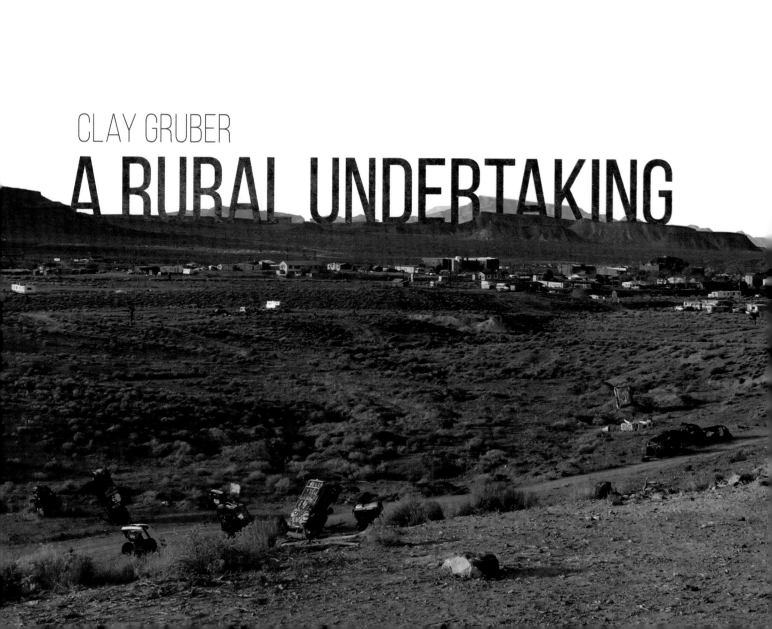

CLAY GRUBER
A RURAL UNDERTAKING

Clay Gruber is a designer based in New York City. He holds graduate degrees in architecture and landscape architecture from the University of Pennsylvania, where he was also a graduate research fellow at Perry World House. His work focuses on the interchange between labor, ecology, and culture as these themes unfold socially and spatially in rural and urban environments.

+ ECONOMICS, DESIGN

Previous: The International Car Forest of the Last Church looking toward Goldfield, Nevada.

Opposite: Views of the town and lithium flats of Silver Peak, Nevada.

After the 2016 US presidential election, a *New York Times* map entitled "The Two Americas of 2016" showed the geographical distribution of the electors who had voted for Hillary Clinton and those who had voted for Donald Trump. Three million square miles of US territory (80%) were deemed "Trump's America" as opposed to only a half a million (15%) considered to be "Hillary's America."[1] Since, pastoral images of America's Heartland have been replaced by a more sinister picture that has enhanced the rural and urban divide. Books like *Hillbilly Elegy* by J.D. Vance, *Strangers In their Own Land* by Arlie Hochschild, and *White Trash: The 400-Year Untold History of Class in America* by Nancy Isenberg have articulated sociological narratives that expose the less than picturesque realities of rural American life. Economic regions once full of vitality and opportunity have become shells of their former selves.

Like the *New York Times* maps, architect and urbanist Rem Koolhaas has looked at rural America through a spatial lens. Shortly after the election, in an interview with *Dezeen*, he remarked, "I was not completely surprised when Trump won... In the last 10 to 15 years we have almost exclusively looked at cities." Koolhaas goes on to wager that "90 or even 99%" of design intelligence in that time has focused exclusively on urban environments.[2] There is, of course, justification for why designers have been so city-centric in the past two decades. Globally, there has been mass rural-to-urban migration and the United Nations now predicts that two-thirds of the world's population will be living in cities and urban areas in the near future.[3] Furthermore, the mainstays of rural economic life have seen major shifts as well. In 1870, 50% of US employment was in the agriculture industry;[4] today, this figure is just 2%.[5]

The once thriving blue collar regions of America have become political hornet's nests scattered throughout the country, characterized by political disaffection, social problems, crumbling infrastructure, and an uncertain future.[6] At the root of these issues is destabilization caused by shifts in industry. We are currently going through a period that Austrian-American economist Joseph Schumpeter would call "creative destruction." For Schumpeter, creative destruction was the essence of capitalism, in which "old forms of industry are continuously being replaced by new ones."[7] The landscape is shaped by these phases: a job, a community, a town, or a forest that is here today will be gone tomorrow. The desolate conditions of former manufacturing cities like Detroit, Michigan, coal towns such as Lynch, Kentucky, and hundreds of abandoned ghost towns scattered across the country are evidence that 20th-century industries have left and are not coming back.

Klaus Schwab, the executive chairman of the World Economic Forum, calls this moment the "fourth industrial revolution" and notes that the speed of its technological development is unprecedented.[8] A 2015 report from McKinsey Global Institute argues that industrial mutation is currently "happening ten times faster and at 300 times the scale, or roughly 3,000 times the impact," of the first Industrial Revolution.[9]

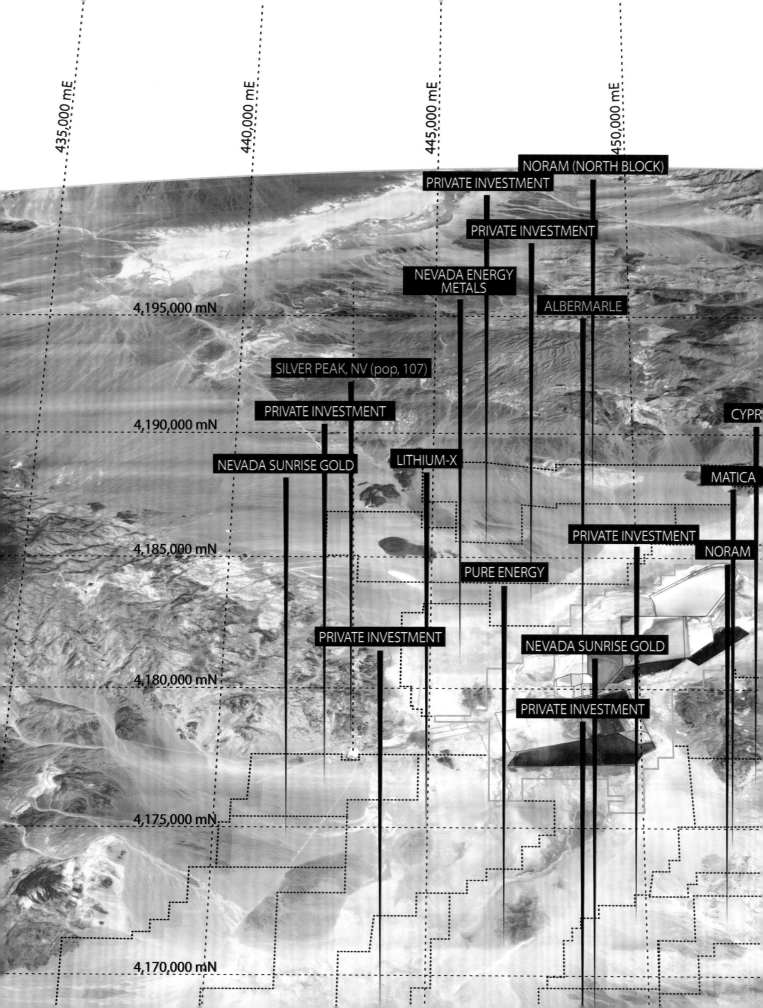

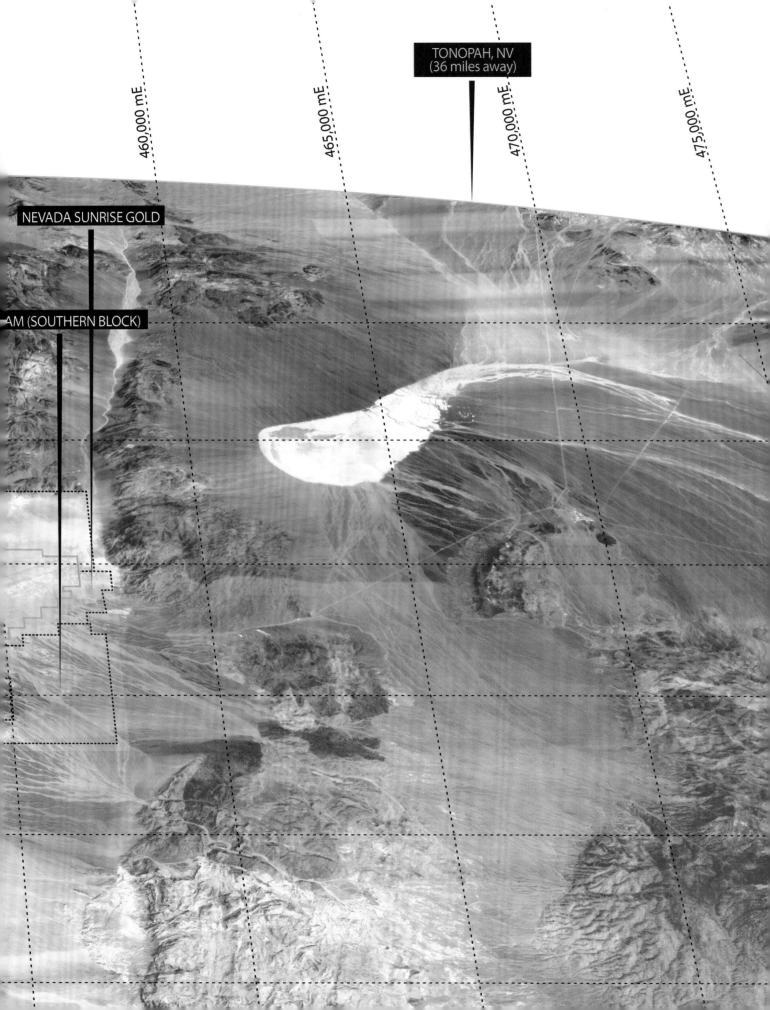

TONOPAH, NV
(36 miles away)

460,000 mE

465,000 mE

470,000 mE

475,000 mE

NEVADA SUNRISE GOLD

AM (SOUTHERN BLOCK)

The long-term implications of the fourth industrial revolution are not well understood but its immediate impact is evident in the townscapes of middle America. The blue-collar jobs of the 19th and early 20th centuries that make up the bulk of rural and suburban employment have been hit the hardest and the consequences have already made a direct political impact. Analysis by Oxford University's Martin School suggests a correlation between those who voted for Donald Trump in 2016 and those who were at the most risk of having their jobs lost due to automation.[10] This research cites a 2014 poll that found that 37% of unemployed Americans between the ages of 25 and 44 stated automation as a primary cause of their economic misfortunes.[11] Furthermore, research by economist Carl Frey and automation engineering specialist Michael Osborne predicts that 47% of US jobs are at risk of being automated by 2030,[12] meaning the political upheaval of the fourth industrial revolution is only just getting started. One of the major hurdles of technological advancement is that the knowledge gap between experts and users has widened to the extent that individuals can no longer see themselves in the world being built around them. Nowhere is this knowledge disparity more evident than for rural populations who are isolated from hubs of higher education and innovation. In 2015, only 19% of rural adults over the age of 25 had a bachelor's degree, as opposed to 33% of urban adults.[13]

An example of this that is of particular interest to Koolhaas is the under construction Tesla Gigafactory being built outside of Reno, Nevada. Telsa's CEO Elon Musk has celebrated the production facility as being the world's largest building per footprint once completed in 2020. The $5 billion building supports Tesla's lithium-ion battery manufacturing, as well as its growing energy division. Musk argues the gigafactory could employ up to 10,000 people once completed.[14] The question for Musk and other boomtown capitalists is whether the companies implicated in 21st-century extraction will leave the same skeletons across the nation as the industrialists before them. Its answer opens the opportunity for designers to develop design scenarios of vitality rather than destruction.

To this end my research looks at a region four hours south of Tesla's Gigafactory in Nevada's Clayton Valley, currently the only operating Lithium mine in the United States. Coincidentally, an hour northwest of the Silver Peak Lithium mine is the Crescent Dune Solar Project, the first of 11 regional solar facilities that the energy company SolarReserve plans to build throughout the next several decades, making it the largest solar project in the world.[15] The combination of these solar projects and the expansion of lithium mining within Clayton Valley will potentially make this region the renewable energy capital of North America.

The largest town in the desolate high desert of central Nevada is Tonopah, a former silver-mining town with a current population of 2,478. Based off SolarReserve's estimated numbers and scaling the current numbers of workers in the Silver Peak mine to the level of lithium prospects for the region, it can be

1 Tim Wallace, "The Two Americas of 2016," *The New York Times* (November 16, 2016), https://www.nytimes.com/interactive/2016/11/16/us/politics/the-two-americas-of-2016.html.

2 Marcus Fairs, "Rem Koolhaas Not Surprised by Donald Trump's Shock Election Win," *Dezeen* (September 29, 2017), https://www.dezeen.com/2016/12/05/rem-koolhaas-donald-trump-usa-presidential-election-not-surprised/.

3 United Nations, "World's Population Increasingly Urban with More than Half Living in Urban Areas | UN DESA Department of Economic and Social Affairs," http://www.un.org/en/development/desa/news/population/world-urbanization-prospects-2014.html (2014).

4 Patricia A. Daily, "Agricultural Employment: Has the Decline Ended?," *US Bureau of Labor Statistics* (November 1981), 12 https://www.bls.gov/opub/mlr/1981/11/art2full.pdf.

5 "Employment by Major Industry Sector," *US Bureau of Labor Statistics* (October 24, 2017), https://www.bls.gov/emp/tables/employment-by-major-industry-sector.htm.

6 "Did You Know? US Infrastructure Is Failing Rural Americans," *The White House* (February 21, 2018), https://www.whitehouse.gov/articles/know-u-s-infrastructure-failing-rural-americans/.

7 Joseph Alois Schumpeter, *Capitalism, Socialism, and Democracy* (New York, NY: Harper Perennial Modern Thought, 2008), 83.

8 Klaus Schwab, *The Fourth Industrial Revolution* (London: Portfolio Penguin, 2017).

9 Richard Dobbs, et al., "The Four Global Forces Breaking All the Trends," https://www.mckinsey.com/business-functions/strategy-and-corporate-finance/our-insights/the-four-global-forces-breaking-all-the-trends.

10 Carl B. Frey, et al., "Political machinery: did robots swing the 2016 US presidential election?," *Oxford Review of Economic Policy* 34, no. 3 (July 2, 2018).

11 L. Hamel, "Kaiser Family Foundation/New York Times/CBS News Non-Employed Poll," (Menlo Park, CA: Kaiser Family Foundation, 2014).

12 Carl B. Frey & Michael A. Osborne. *The Future of Employment: How Susceptible Are Jobs to Computerization* (Oxford: Oxford Martin School, 2013), 37–38.

13 US Department of Agriculture (USDA), "Rural Education," https://www.ers.usda.gov/topics/rural-economy-population/employment-education/rural-education/.

Previous: A map of the existing Albermarle Lithium Mine, and additional lithium claims to undeveloped land throughout the Clayton Valley.

Opposite: At the turn of the 20th century Tonopah was one of the wealthiest and most prolific silver-mining towns in the American west.

estimated that around 3,800 workers will enter the region within the next decade only to leave within a 20-year timeframe when minerals are exhausted and related employment wanes.[16] The question I have asked in my research is whether the energy of the boom can be used in preparation for bust; that is, whether Tonopah can become a better place for both its temporary and, more importantly, its permanent residents. Put another way, I ask whether the 19th-century idea of the company town can be applied productively to the 21st century and if so, how?

To begin, I argue that the first role of the designer in the 21st-century boomtown is to act as an intermediary between incoming private companies and the public sector. This is a form of masterplanning in which design decisions capitalize on a temporary influx of financing, access to innovative technology, and jobs training that companies like SolarReserve will bring to the region. This requires decisions that determine what elements of the boomtown development stay after industry leaves and what goes. In Tonopah, collaborative investment by both lithium and solar interests in a community center and jobs training facility in the middle of the town services both private and public interests during the boom, while transitioning to a community hub run by the city once industry leaves town. As well, medical facilities and other general amenities need to be established at the onset of the boom, given that the closest medical center to Tonopah is over 200 miles away.

Once community and industrial amenities are accounted for, an inventory of vacant land, housing stock, and existing landscape conditions (such as, topography and hydrologic features) needs to be established to account for the expansion and contraction of a doubling or tripling of the town's current size. This process takes ingenuity, as designers need to determine where to locate permanent housing, as well as plan and design for flexible housing typologies and infrastructure. Moreover, these decisions need to consider how new development can leave or be repurposed after the bust with the most minimal impact on the land and community.

The boom also brings with it tools and technology expertise that would have previously cost an exorbitant amount of money to ship to the region. The temporary proximity of these assets to Tonopah along with an increased tax base, allow for the city to invest in infrastructural updates that will make the town resilient in the 21st century. In practical terms, the high desert environment of central Nevada requires investment in water capture and harvesting, as well as turning the grid over to being supported by solar energy.

Perhaps one of the most important elements of bringing 21st-century technology into rural landscapes is how access and proximity to these technologies demystifies our current moment of industrial mutation. As members of a given household return home with training in solar technology or computer programming, families begin to see themselves in the evolution of 21st-century society. The built environment needs do the same; not through the futuristic curved polycarbonate forms of its urban counterparts, but through subtle pragmatic gestures that enhance the population's quality of life. Solar-powered street lamps, technologically advanced urban agriculture practices, and inexpensive infrastructural upgrades prove the process and value of technological upgrades to a skeptical public, rather than its vanity and unfamiliarity.

This design work becomes extremely important for both private and public parties. For private companies, particularly ones who deal in extraction and energy, the public has increasingly demanded accountability for the environmental

and social impact their work has on the land and communities they affect. So much so, that our digitally connected world has taken accountability global, requiring the Ayn Randian industrialists to soften their approach and adopt a benevolent ethos. This creates an opportunity for local governments to work with companies to bring much-needed financing into rural communities that have been struggling to create healthy, livable environments.

As Rem Koolhaas argues, "If you look carefully, the countryside is changing much more rapidly and radically than the 'city.'"[17] Yet, this radical change has gone unnoticed by the design community. By looking into how the 21st century is changing our rural environments, we will find opportunities for designers to breathe vitality back into the neglected corners of our world. The consequence of which will only enhance the vitality of our own professions. Entering nearly unexplored territories for the first time, designers have real opportunities to strengthen communities, create new forms of collaborating, and expand our existing toolkits. Opening our eyes to the lost corners of the country by redefining the 21st-century boomtown will be a good place to start.

14 Fred Lambert, "Tesla Gigafactory Now Employs Over 850 Workers, 1,000 More to Come in First Half of 2017 with Production Ramp Up," https://electrek.co/2016/12/08/tesla-gigafactory-workers-2017-production-ramp-up/ [December 9, 2016].

15 Joe Ryan, "SolarReserve Planning World's Largest Solar Farm for $5 Billion," *Bloomberg* [October 13, 2016] https://www.bloomberg.com/news/articles/2016-10-13/solarreserve-plans-world-s-largest-solar-farm-for-5-billion.

16 SolarReserve, "Sandstone" https://www.solarreserve.com/en/global-projects/csp/sandstone; Rockstone Research, "Prima Diamond Acquires the Green Energy Project in Utah with Historic Lithium Grades of 1700 Mg per Liter," http://rockstone-research.com/index.php/en/research-reports/667-Prima-Diamond-Acquires-the-Green-Energy-Project-in-Utah-with-Historic-Lithium-Grades-of-1700-mg-per-liter.

17 Rem Koolhaas, "Rem Koolhaas Sees the Future in the Countryside," *The Economist* [2018], http://www.theworldin.com/edition/2018/article/14595/rem-koolhaas-sees-future-countryside.

Below: Cemetery at Goldfield, Nevada.

"I don't pretend I know what happens next."
Ethan Hawke, *I Know Annie*

Mindy Thompson Fullilove is a professor of urban policy and health at The New School, New York. She previously worked as a research psychiatrist at New York State Psychiatric Institute and as a professor of clinical psychiatry and public health at Columbia University. She has conducted research on AIDS and other epidemics of poor communities, with a special interest in the relationship between the collapse of communities and decline in health. Fullilove is author of a number of books including *Root Shock: How Tearing Up City Neighborhoods Hurts America and What We Can Do About It* (2nd ed. 2016), and *Urban Alchemy: Restoring Joy in America's Sorted-Out Cities* (2013).

╋ URBAN DESIGN, LITERATURE, ART

Above: Pierre Perron's *Le Cortège de l'an*, 2000.

I've been observing Main Streets for 10 years, a quest which started with idle curiosity about their liveliness. It occurred to me that, though people said Main Streets are dead, there were lots of lively Main Streets, like the one where I was drinking coffee and watching the crowds pass as I had the thought. If Main Streets are alive, I thought, they help our mental health in some way, but how? I decided I would visit Main Street in 100 cities to find out about this.

One problem I've had thinking about Main Street this past year is the metaphor I've been using – I think of it as a kind of shoebox, with buildings as sides, the street as the bottom, sky as the top, and short open sides punctuated by gas stations so that we know when it's over. I knew I was missing something. My urbanism teacher, Michel Cantal-Dupart, once said, "I organized my bergerie as a house in the country, but if I had thought of it as a boat, I would have made better decisions." Like many of his teaching stories, I didn't understand until I saw the little place, just off of the road, where he and his family passed the summers. In that wooded place, you wouldn't think "boat," but it was a better model for making a tiny building efficient for a lot of people.

I decided to tape 50 or so Main Street photos on the walls of my office: the Christmas Market in Berlin, Times Square, Bernie Sanders strolling with the heifers in Brattleboro, sweeping down a hill to enter Englewood, NJ, and the crumbling ruins of Old Town Mall in Baltimore. I looked at each as an old friend, a reminder of a day and a visit that I held in my heart and mind. But one day I stopped and asked: what are you all saying to me? As I paused, I saw the collection showing me a single gesture of the street: the allée, which in landscape design is the lining of a street or path with trees, but in the case of Main Street means the sides are made of buildings, giving form to the sweep of the roadway.

The New York Times published a special report on Main Streets with chunks of empty stores and homeless people moving into the empty spaces not needed by the respectable among us.[1] I have been seeing that emptiness, and it worried me, like the death of the American elm from an upheaval in our ecology, the end of the great allées arched by their splendid curving branches. Even Main Streets that had survived the malls–even Main Streets lining rich neighborhoods–are falling to some combination of the concentration of wealth, internet shopping, and gentrification. It doesn't take much to destroy the architecture of the allée.

It was Cantal who introduced me to Pierre Perron, who has been lucky to live in art all his life, taking delight in sly jokes and games he could make from everyday happenings. For the millennium, when we feared the rupture of time, he envisioned *Le cortège de l'an 2000*, an allée of dancing ancestors going back many generations so that we might stroll within the continuity of their lives just as the clock stood at 11:59:59. The world had talked so much of that second that I held my breath, a little shocked when it sailed smoothly, unhesitatingly past and we could all yell "Happy New Year!" just as we always did. I saw Perron's ancestors that summer and let go of the last remnants of my fear.

Michael Lally writes of my people–we of exit 145, The Oranges and Newark–just as I know us to be, and so I think he is the greatest poet in the world. His 2018 book, *Another Way to Play*, has a blurb by writer and poet Bob Holman on the back. It says, "He's our Walt Whitman. And this is his *Leaves of Grass*."[2] That makes me cry, imagining the crest of a wave that once caught Whitman, and has now lifted Lally so that he can see and we can know. As Perron knows, two points make a line, a continuity that we can rest within, finding the intricacy of the dance. They form an allée and offer a new way to understand Main Street.

Lally is our Whitman from the magnitude of his voice, the sexiness of his oeuvre, and the attention to the people he lives among. From Whitman's *Leaves of Grass*, we find this set of verses:

```
        The boatmen and clam-diggers arose early and stopt for me,
    I tuck'd my trowser-ends in my boots and went and had a good time;
    You should have been with us that day round the chowder-kettle.

    I saw the marriage of the trapper in the open air in the far west,
                    the bride was a red girl…

        The runaway slave came to my house and stopt outside,
          I heard his motions crackling the twigs of the woodpile,
    Through the swung half-door of the kitchen I saw him limpsy and weak,
        And went where he sat on a log and led him in and assured him,
    And brought water and fill'd a tub for his sweated body and bruis'd feet,
  And gave him a room that enter'd from my own, and gave him some coarse clean clothes,
        And remember perfectly well his revolving eyes and his awkwardness,
        And remember putting plasters on the galls of his neck and ankles;
      He staid with me a week before he was recuperated and pass'd north,
        I had him sit next me at table, my fire-lock lean'd in the corner.³
```

In the sense of Perron's allée, Whitman's friends–the clamdiggers, trappers, and runaway slaves–are now our ancestors. It is perhaps *November Sonnet* that helps us see the continuity between Whitman's then and Lally's now:

```
On a perfectly clear Fall day, heading back to
   Fort Monmouth, I watched as other cars on
    The Garden State Parkway veered onto the
   shoulder and stopped; the drivers not getting
 out, just sitting there. At the toll booth the man
    said The president's been shot. As I drove on,
  more cars pulled off the road. I could see their
     drivers weeping. Back in the barracks we stayed
    in the rec room watching the black and white
    TV, tension in the room like static. When they
      named Lee Harvey Oswald, I watched the
   black guys hold their breath, hoping that meant
     redneck, not spade, and every muscle in their
      faces relax when he turned out to be white.[4]
```

The great-great-great-grandbabies of the runaway slave, the trapper, the clamdiggers might have been with Lally at Fort Monmouth or sobbing in a car he passed by the side of the highway. And we would know what they were feeling by a twitch or a smile, just as the poets remind us we do.

Whitman was writing *Leaves of Grass* in 1855 – singing the body electric when it seemed everybody else was hiding behind metaphor, under the thumb of the Calvinists. But maybe Whitman is telling us what was really going on, that lots of people were singing the body electric and he was partying with all of them. He wrote:

```
   I dote on myself, there is that lot of me and all so luscious,
      Each moment and whatever happens thrills me with joy,
 I cannot tell how my ankles bend, nor whence the cause of my faintest wish,
    Nor the cause of the friendship I emit, nor the cause of the
                   friendship I take again.
```

Lally is absolutely pleased to embrace the sensual, spell it out for us, remind us that we know our own body electric. Like Whitman, he offers to us desire and its partner, satisfaction. In *Loving Women*, he details a bus ride home from spending time with a girl he'd just met and fallen in love with:

```
     My shirt was unbuttoned down to the
        fifth buttonhole and my hairless
        teenaged chest was exposed enough
      to see that right between my little
        male tits was the imprint of two
      bright red lips—a lipstick tattoo.

      It almost glowed the way I flaunted
     it, showed them all what I'd been up
        to and was proud of, proud to be a
      teenager when that word was only one
      step removed from monster or moron,
        criminal or alien being—or love.
```

The poets get in our face about the small and large dramas of life, and this is what we have to reconcile with Main Street. Box doesn't work. It is too mechanical, emphasizing what is there, its dimensions and utilities. Box makes us think it is about retail and without stores Main Street will die. Main Streets do die, but they don't die because of what stores do. Like the elms, they collapse because the ecology has shifted and the conditions they need for survival are no longer there.

A Main Street is an allée, a way that is part drama and part quotidian. While passing through, we get to look at one another, to sing, to recognize what we are, have been, might be. Main Streets might cease to be the way we find our collective selves. Whitman went to bull dances in the fields, Lally to clubs – different and yet not. Perron's allée, alive with generations, is the truth of Main Street. It is the metaphor that I was missing, distracted by my own method, which was to go to Main Street, have lunch, shop. It took a long time before I could see all those Main Streets on my wall, recognize the force of the pathway leading us to the horizon, put matters in perspective, shaped as it is by brick and mortar, and see that the people dancing down its streets were the message – Main Street is simply the medium of our times.

Right on the heels of the spread on the death of retail, *The New York Times* arrived at my house sheathed in a shiny black section. I pulled the paper out of its blue plastic bag and read on the glossy back paper, THE DEATH OF RETAIL—I had to open it to the inside to continue—IS OVERRATED. It invited us to a new shopping experience right by the High Line, at this moment a favorite site for the dance.

Whitman left this call to the poets who would follow, to Lally as we can see:

```
        Poets to come! orators, singers, musicians to come!
      Not to-day is to justify me and answer what I am for,
But you, a new brood, native, athletic, continental, greater than before known,
            Arouse! for you must justify me.
```

Main Streets are the same way, always changing, and we don't know what happens next, except we do know that, as long as there are people, they will find a place to sing the body electric. Let the future answer what we are for.

1 Corey Kilgannon, "The Space Available," Special Report, *The New York Times* (September 2, 2018).

2 Michael Lally, *Another Way to Play: Poems 1960–2017* (New York: Seven Stories Press, 2018).

3 The Guttenberg Files are the source of the quotes from Walt Whitman's *Leaves of Grass*. The text can be found at https://www.gutenberg.org/files/1322/1322-h/1322-h.htm#link2H_4_0030. "Limpsy" is dialectal and means limp, especially from lack of physical strength. A "fire-lock" is a gun having a lock in which the priming is ignited by sparks struck from flint and steel, as the flintlock musket.

4 Michael Lally's poems quoted here are taken, with permission, from *Another Way to Play*.

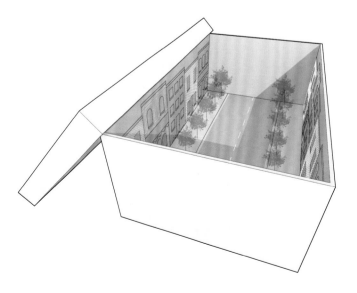

IN CONVERSATION WITH

JANE BENNETT

While architecture takes flight, landscape architecture is of the ground. Traditionally, this ground has anchored both the peasant and poet against the centrifuge of modernity, but now the ground itself is full of toxins and detritus "made by man." So, if it is no longer possible to innocently love this ground, it is incumbent upon us to continue to breathe vitality into it. For this we need first to find new words for old ground. Someone who designers have turned to for these words is the North American political philosopher, and author of *Vibrant Matter: The Political Ecology of Things*, Jane Bennett. **Richard Weller** interviewed Bennett on behalf of *LA+ Journal*.

+ Your 2010 book *Vibrant Matter* begins with an epiphany as you stare into a puddle of urban detritus in Baltimore. From this unlikely wellspring, you construct an aesthetics and a politics of ecology that challenges the modern (Cartesian) scientific and economic worldview of nature as an inert resource. Can you briefly retrace that arc for us?

It's less an arc than a wavy line with switchbacks, but the trajectory was, as you say, toward the revival of a (not so) minor tradition of Euro-American thought, according to which materials were really *felt* to be lively, (quasi) independent forces. These forces were experienced as being operative in nature and also in (though not wholly "of") human beings. The propelling insight of *Vibrant Matter* was nothing special: it was simply that even today (in a modern world defined as "disenchanted"), ordinary experience includes moments where so-called inanimate stuff tugs at our sleeves, calls out, enables us to act, and trips us up in flows not wholly of our making or wholly susceptible to rational or technical control. Acknowledging *limits* to human mastery is a necessary first step toward crafting more effective collaborations with stuff that has its *own* persistent tendencies and activities. It turns out that human efforts aiming to vanquish rival forces are often less effective than those seeking to form productive if uneasy assemblages with them. (Do not wage a war of annihilation with the HIV virus but keep its viral load below the point where it overwhelms the well-being of the virus-flesh assemblage. Thanks to Jairus Grove for that example. Or, as Deleuze and Guattari said in *A Thousand Plateaus* "form a rhizome with our viruses, or rather our viruses cause us to form a rhizome with other animals.")

+ In *Vibrant Matter* you ask, "What would happen to our thinking about nature if we experienced materialities as actants, and how would the direction of public policy shift if it attended more carefully to their trajectories and powers?" What are the trajectories and powers you refer to, and how might we attend to them more carefully?

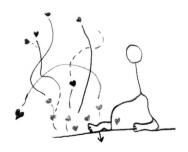

Walt Whitman's *Leaves of Grass* (currently my favorite book) helps me to name one of those "powers" – specifically, a kind of gravitational or connective power (one could call it a radically *apersonal* "sympathy") by which bodies become drawn into each other's orbit. The example comes from these two lines of his "Song of Myself."

> The press of my foot springs a hundred affections.
> They scorn the best I can do to relate them.

Here, Whitman refigures the act of taking a step as an *encounter* between foot and ground, where ground too presents itself as a player – as a site and a prompt for "affections." These affections are irreducible to the sentiment of the human walker. They are apersonal, atmospheric *currents* springing up between a sensitive foot and a gravity-saturated, moist, and vibratory geo-surface of Earth. These affections are more "affects" than emotions. They "go beyond the strength of those who undergo them," say Deleuze and Guattari in *What is Philosophy?*

This swarm of affections "scorns" rational comprehension. Human attempts to identify a stable system of relations between the "hundred affections" get bounced back. Also confounded is any attempt to distinguish sharply between cause and effect: the "press of my foot" is, well, mine – or is it the pulling down of gravity? Likewise, the "spring" is a function of foot lifted by walker *and* the (spring-back) resistance offered by the ground. The odd syntax of the line—"the press of my foot springs" rather than "from the press of my foot springs"—shows human foot, earthly gravity, and affections to be sprung *together*, quickened into life by virtue of their encounter.

Messages I take from this example: human and nonhuman "powers" are always entangled; humans are Earthlings. The example is both poetic and prosaic, for it illustrates something very basic about life, more basic than what the language of "public policy" is able to articulate.

How did Whitman even *notice* the existence of these apersonal trajectories and atmospheric powers? By practicing a technique that he calls "doting." Doting is a cultivated style of perceiving and describing; it is a highly sensitive "loafing" that luxuriates in the encounter without judging it. It inhabits an interval, which delays judgment. Doting relies upon what Deleuze and Guattari call (in *A Thousand Plateaus*) the power of the "little detail that starts to swell and carries you off."

The poems model this doting in the hope that the practice will mimetically infect the reader's own style of encounter. The object of Whitman's doting includes himself ("I dote on myself, there is that lot of me and all so luscious"), but doting is an appropriate posture toward all kinds of things, including:

```
The blab of the pave, tires of carts, sluff of boot-soles, talk of the promenaders,
       The heavy omnibus, the driver with his interrogating thumb,
            the clank of the shod horses on the granite floor,
       The snow-sleighs, clinking, shouted jokes, pelts of snow-ball,
                                ...
            What living and buried speech is always vibrating here...
```

Pave and promenader, clanks and jokes – each is worthy of dote because each "vibrates" and "speaks." Doting allows Whitman to sense the physicality of the impression things make, where the word "impression" refers not solely to a mental or psychological image, but also to an outside pressing in and *making a dent* on a body.

A lot depends on what one has in mind when invoking "the political." Today, that most often conjures up a realm of antagonisms, strife, conflict. In 2018 and continuing to this new year, American politics is marked by hate, racism, misogyny, xenophobia, disdain for the rule of law, private and corporate greed, unprecedented concentration of wealth, ruthless indifference toward the suffering of others, and belligerent denial of that profound, albeit unequally distributed, precarity that is climate change. All of this finds a powerful advocate in a president who spins them as forms of self-defense and national pride. These stances and efforts, however, are met by forceful and livid opposition, by a pro-democratic, anti-racist counter-politics of direct action, mass protest, legal challenge, electoral strategizing, and militant *calling out* of entrenched structures of privilege and domination.

I too think that anti-democratic and fascist flows must be met with strong and unrelenting opposition. My writing, however, tends to highlight another set of pro-democratic ["political"] practices and tactics. It leans into moods other than outrage, revulsion, and agonism. It dotes, for example, on wonder at the vitality of matter and on the operative presence of a protean tendency for bodies to make connections and form attachments. I am keen to explore the possibility that human wonder and vague, ahuman "affections" might be harnessed on behalf of a generous, egalitarian, ecological public culture. I don't view such discerning "enchantments" as a replacement for agonistic opposition, but as an indispensable "political" supplement to it. Thus the dominant rhetorical groove in my writing is less a calling out than a calling in and a calling toward. And for some audiences, this renders my perspective and my efforts un-political. But I don't think so, especially if by "political" one means to invoke and harness positive energies capable of engendering social transformation.

Why focus on the vibrancy of matter or cultivate a sensibility of doting? Because neglect of such experiential styles made its own contribution to the rise of the neo-fascist, Earth-destroying politics we now endure. I seek to add a non-agonistic set of practices to the political mix. As my friend Kathy Ferguson says, the work of change always needs a discordant chorus, "because we have multiple audiences, because different trajectories work together in unexpected ways, because we should never put all our eggs in just one basket."

With regard to the movement in the US, a couple of points come to mind.[1] First, I have been surprised at the enduring appeal of what is often dismissed as a "pastoral" image of nature, the one exemplified, for example, by Thoreau. A longing for quiet, relatively open spaces, with lots of green plants and birdsong and (not too many) small nonhuman mammals, still seems to have motivational power even among those of us who officially affirm a non-providential cosmos (as per Val Plumwood's claim in "Being Prey" that people live in a "Heraclitean universe" where we serve as food for other beings, or Foucault's claim that we "must not suppose that the world turns to us a legible face" in his "Discourse on Language.")

+ Are the political ramifications of a heightened awareness of materiality revolutionary and/or utopian and if so in what way?

+ As a philosopher and political theorist what is your assessment of the environmental movement as it has evolved over the course of the last century or so?

Second, I note the "nonhuman turn," by which eco-activists and scholars try to (in the words of Richard Grusin's introduction in a volume of essays by that title) "decenter the human in favor of a...concern for the nonhuman, understood variously in terms of animals, affectivity, bodies, organic and geophysical systems, materiality, or technology." The nonhuman turn does not exclude altogether a Thoreau-style phenomenology that accents how the out-of-doors makes (some) people *feel* refreshed and disturbed as outside influences rewire their central nervous systems. But it does place those effects alongside less *benevolent* nonhuman agencies and outcomes.

+ An increasingly urbanized global body-politic seems evermore estranged from intimacy with the material flows of things. How do we breathe more material vitality into our cities?

Architects, urban planners, and artists know much more than I do about how to dramatize in spatial forms the ongoing vitality of nonhuman materials (e.g., Meret Oppenheim's famous moss- and ice-covered fountain in Bern). I will just list some already-well-known efforts that, in my home city of Baltimore, have been successful in highlighting an often subtle but real efficacy of materialities, and in forging counter-hegemonic channels of movement:

- The restoration of urban streams and rivers that had been forced underground or had their banks paved with concrete.

- The addition of exclusive bike lanes to city streets in order to reclaim without apology some territory back from automobility.

- Urban walking tours oriented around wild plants and litter or trash, so that people can learn to sense vibrations that are vegetal, mineral, and plastic. Here I cite Marisa Prefer's "Weed walks: wild plants, queer landscapes."[2] Trash is ubiquitous in cities: can we find ways to feel more acutely the affects induced in us by all that stuff, to better sense the way it sets a mood (of callousness or of wonder) or reminds us of what we have been eating and doing? References here might include Anand Pandian's "Plastic"[3] or an essay Alex Livingston and I wrote for *Scapegoat Journal* called "Philosophy in the Wild: Listening to Things in Baltimore."

+ You write that, "Sometimes ecohealth will require individuals and collectives to back off or ramp down their activeness and sometimes it will call for grander more dramatic and violent expenditures of human energy." Could you provide some examples of what you mean?

I have already gestured toward a ramping-down of a *restless* and *judging* kind of activeness in my discussion of Whitman and doting. For an example of a more dramatic and oppositional expenditure of human energy, I turn to my partner and colleague William Connolly's call in *Facing the Planetary* for a "cross-regional general strike" in response to the mortal threat that is climate change:

"Such a strike will involve withdrawal from work and travel joined to mass reductions of consumption above the levels needed for subsistence. It will also be marked by intensive lobbying of key institutions, such as legislatures, churches, unions, universities, corporations, farmers, foundations, retirement funds, parties, international agencies, and localities. The cross-regional action could be enacted for a defined period on the first occasion...with a promise to renew it if the relevant institutions do not initiate a specified series of interim actions. The actions demanded could include promises of a rapid shift in the eco-priorities of numerous nonstate institutions, radical state and local projects to reorganize the power grid, a radical reorientation of subsidies in the infrastructure of consumption, action to relieve debt in third world countries and student life, support for worker collectives, financial support by the old capitalist states of other regions seeking to undertake eco-actions, media publicity to reorient the public ethos of investment and consumption, and hundreds of billions...from rich to poor countries that have suffered inordinate damage."[4]

Connolly says quite clearly that the odds of such a strike happening are low: "So let's agree that such an event is improbable." But time is short and the real question is what will happen if we *don't* try to induce something as unlikely as a general strike. We need to focus on making improbabilities like this into live possibilities.

Along with Connolly, Rom Coles (in *Visionary Pragmatism* and elsewhere) makes a persuasive case, for a politics that combines the receptive and the militant. There are, he says, "myriad immanent relationships between the political ecology of sympathies, and associated militant struggles that are sometimes necessary to defend and amplify sympathetic associations."[5]

+ What are you working on now?

A book with the provisional title of "Influx & Efflux: Writing up with Walt Whitman." If *Vibrant Matter* accented the efforts of non- or not-quite-human shapes, arguing that the modern habit of parsing the world into passive matter (its) and vibrant life (us) had the effect of understating nonhuman powers and trajectories, the new project tries to depict, amidst a world of diverse powers and trajectories, that particular effort that has an intimately local, personal feel. What kind of "I" can exist in a world of vibrant matter? How to theorize the value-added, the extra oomph, impetus, or effort, of dividuated human beings (without reverting to a self-enclosed purely human model of subjectivity)? *Influx & Efflux* explores the experience of being continuously subject to outside influences and still managing to add something to the mix.

The new book is inspired by Whitman, but also by my lifelong practice of doodling. Is the doodle following rules of some geometry, or does it emerge in real time without a plan, each vague shape engendering a next on the fly? And what is *my* role in doodling? It seems I add something to the aesthetic of what also has the feel of automatic writing. The doodle is somehow subjective without being the expression of a pure interiority all my own. Researchers have shown how doodling helps people to think, to process ideas. But doodling sparked my current project in another way, too: the peculiar experience of self that comes to the fore while doodling—an "I" at once receptive and creative—became a key theme to explore.

1 For discussions of the eco-movements in other geographies, I rely, among others, upon Serenella Iovino's 2016 *Ecocriticism and Italy: Ecology, Resistance, and Liberation*, Willy Blomme's discussion of "Printemps Érable" in Canada in the blog *The Contemporary Condition*, Anatoli Ignatov's *Political Theory* essay "The Earth as a Gift-Giving Ancestor: Nietzschean Perspectivism and African Animism," and Stephanie Erev's doctoral dissertation "Earthly Considerations" at Johns Hopkins on nonhuman agencies, gardening, and political action in the work of Antiguan-American Jamaica Kincaid.

2 See, https://invisiblelabor.org.

3 See, https://culanth.org/fieldsights/795-plastic.

4 William Connolly, *Facing the Planetary* (Durham, NC: Duke University Press, 2017), 144–45.

5 Romand Coles, "Walt Whitman, Jane Bennett, and the Paradox of Antagonistic Sympathy," *Political Research Quarterly* 69, no. 3 (2016), 621–25, at 624.

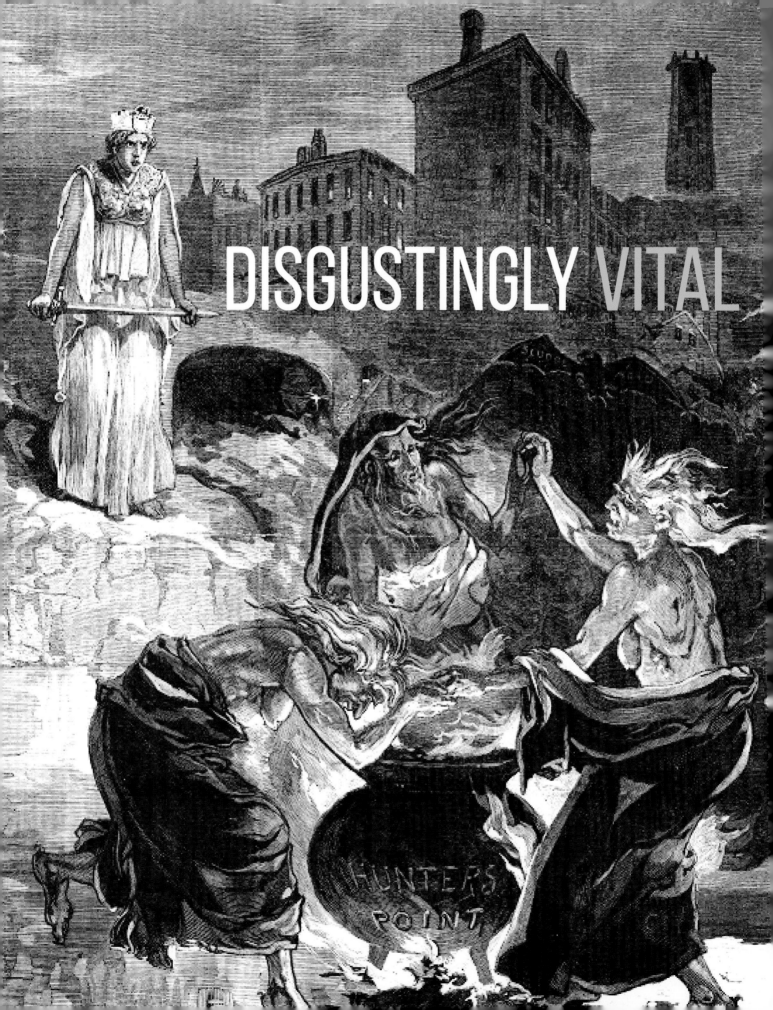

DISGUSTINGLY VITAL

COLIN CURLEY

Colin Curley is a designer based in New York City, where he is an associate at James Corner Field Operations. His design research explores the complex environmental and sociopolitical dimensions of hyper-toxic industrial landscapes and their aesthetic and experiential potential. Curley holds a Master of Landscape Architecture and Master of Architecture from the University of Pennsylvania, and a Bachelor of Science in Architecture from the University of Virginia.

+ URBAN ECOLOGY, AESTHETICS

"The biggest fear suggested by the contemporary technological landscape is the death of humanity in the midst of the signs of its triumph over nature."[1]

In New York City, chances are that the waste one throws away, recycles, or flushes down a toilet will at some point pass through the Newtown Creek. It is the proverbial "elsewhere" – the place where one can find everything considered better off out-of-sight and out-of-mind. Home to the largest wastewater treatment plant in New York City, metal scrap yards, recycling and sanitation facilities, and fuel storage depots, the creek has been described as "the moat of man-made filth separating Brooklyn and Queens."[2]

Indeed, the Newtown Creek has been derided in social and political commentary for centuries. An 1870 "Map of Odor Producing Industries" illustrated neighborhoods in Manhattan claiming to be affected by odors carried from the Newtown Creek, while a contemporaneous political cartoon in *Harper's Magazine* depicted a group of witches huddled around a cauldron labeled "Hunter's Point" while a bat with the words "Sludge Acid" on its wings hovers above.[3] And yet, a 1921 advertisement leveraged this characterization to laud the opportunity that the Newtown Creek presented for manufacturers who "ordinarily believe there is no location near the center of the New York district [for industries] whose processes are noisy, dusty, odorous, or in some other way likely to be obnoxious."[4] Today, this characterization is reflected in the zoning of the Newton Creek area, which is specifically designated for use by heavy industries that generate "noise, traffic, or pollutants."[5]

There is no question that industry and urbanization have irrevocably altered the Newtown Creek. Originally a tidal estuary where freshwater from inland areas mixed with brackish water from the East River and flushed out through tidal exchange, combined sewer outfalls (CSOs) have now wholly replaced freshwater inputs, and tidal exchange is essentially nonexistent. The excessive richness

Opposite: An 1881 illustration from *Harpers Magazine* comments on the state of pollution at Hunter's Point on the northern bank of Newtown Creek.

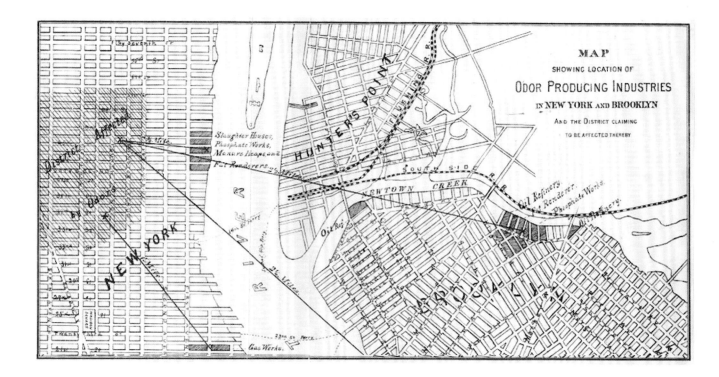

of nutrients introduced by CSOs has led, perhaps inevitably, to eutrophication with algal blooms spreading throughout the creek, significantly reducing levels of dissolved oxygen and rendering the water unable to support marine animals. In addition, the sewershed of the Newtown Creek Wastewater Treatment Plant far exceeds the territory of the creek's watershed and there is virtually no stormwater infrastructure anywhere along its shoreline; as a result, nearly every inch of rain that falls onto the industrial parcels surrounding the Newtown Creek is directly conveyed into its waters.[6] Augmenting this contamination, over the past century between 17 and 30 million gallons of oil from the former ExxonMobil refinery in Greenpoint, Brooklyn percolated into the area's soil and groundwater, forming an approximately 50-acre underground oil plume that has been leaching into the Newtown Creek.[7] In 2010, the Newtown Creek was designated a federal Superfund site, meaning that its contamination is so severe relative to other polluted sites in the United States that its remediation was deemed a national priority.

When presented with a "denatured," disturbed site like the Newtown Creek, landscape architects, as well as the public, generally mobilize to reclaim and restore. Indeed, landscape architects often herald themselves as the heroic agents who reintroduce "nature" into such places. If you Google the search terms "landscape architect breathes life," you will be met with more than 28 million results.

To date, the approach toward the Newtown Creek has been consistent with the reclaim and restore modus operandi. Community groups have called for the wholesale removal and disposal of all contaminated sediment as part of the Superfund cleanup, and restoration of the creek's water to "swimmable levels regarding contamination."[8] As would be expected of any waterfront landscape architectural project, the vision plan imagery depicts verdant shorelines, wetlands, waterfront esplanades, boardwalks, and parks with trellises and amphitheaters.[9] A predictable strategy begets predictable results. But at about four miles from mouth to end, the extent of the Newtown Creek is vast, and the challenges it presents are far more complex than such Photoshopped imagery might suggest.

It is important to acknowledge at least one key assumption implicit within the impulse to reclaim and restore: that there is a clear definition of and distinction between nature and the condition of its absence. Disturbed sites like the Newtown Creek problematize this notion, as they exist in a purgatorial state between being fully alive and completely dead; it is difficult to discern where contamination ends and resilient natural systems begin. Eutrophication is one phenomenon that embodies this tension: the success of one form of life leads to the death of another as a result of human intervention. This disturbs us because it upsets our understanding of how waterways should look and smell, and what is supposed to live in them. It also disturbs us because the impacts of our influence

are rendered palpable, as the opening quote to this article from Antoine Picon's "Anxious Landscapes" suggests. The term "disturbed" therefore refers both to the characterization of these sites and the way they make us feel.[10] The experiential dimension of these sites also envelops aesthetics – as Picon describes them, they are "irreparably polluted yet somehow endowed with a strange beauty."[11]

At the core of our discomfort with disturbed sites and the "strange beauty" they bear is disgust. A strong emotion that prompts a visceral reaction, disgust is used to designate "otherness" and to cast moral judgment. In fact, one's sensitivity to disgust may strongly correlate with political and societal views.[12] Morally speaking, anthropologist Mary Douglas argued that societal order is created by the punishment of transgression and exaggeration of the differences between binary relationships.[13] Following this logic, reclaiming or restoring a disturbed site by any means necessary would be considered a virtuous act. When applied to aesthetics, however, disgust harbors a paradoxical magnetism – inasmuch as it repels, it also has the ability to attract. There are a variety of emotions that can be provoked by aesthetic disgust, including fascination and pleasure.[14]

The design response to the Newtown Creek has followed the "virtuous" path of restoration by any means necessary. Rather than consider the possibility that certain species may

Above: An 1870 map of showing the location of oil refineries and other "odor producing industries" in the vicinity of Newtown Creek (left); photographs of expressions of disgust from Charles Darwin's *The Expression of Emotions in Man and Animals* (right).

Next: Newtown Creek today, as photographed by local artist Mitch Waxman, https://newtownpentacle.com.

be better adapted than others to particular environments at certain points in time, New York City has doubled down on its efforts to eradicate eutrophication. It has installed mechanical aeration systems in English Kills and East Branch, the farthest inland reaches of the Newtown Creek. In the summer, when eutrophication is at its peak, the creek bubbles and foams as though it were a backyard hot tub. Further, rather than embrace the particularities and peculiarities of the Newtown Creek and the strange, austere beauty with which it is endowed, the vision plan depicts a landscape that could be anywhere and seems geared toward commodification and eventual rezoning.[15]

Implementing mechanical aeration and producing verdant renderings that masquerade as restoration may seem at odds with one another, but they have one thing in common: they are both predicated on an evaluation of today's Newtown Creek against the environmental performance and appearance of its precondition. Because the Newtown Creek was originally a tidal estuary, there is a foregone conclusion that it must therefore resemble and harbor the forms of life endemic to a tidal estuary once again. This begs the question whether we are more afraid of how the Newtown Creek functions, or simply how it looks. But why fear either? Toxicity and mutation and the disgust they elicit are a reality of our present, and a condition of our future. Inasmuch as we have created the landscapes of cities, we have also been complicit in the formation of the landscapes of waste and infrastructure that support them.

It is certainly easier to buy into a worldview that suggests there is a way that urban water bodies are *supposed to be*. It is also easier to continue thinking that our waste passes through an enigmatic and placeless "elsewhere." But elsewhere is always

1 Antoine Picon, "Anxious Landscapes: From the Ruin to Rust," *Grey Room* 1 (2000): 79.

2 "Newtown Creek Shows Signs of Poop-Fueled 'Superfood,'" *Gothamist*, http://gothamist. com/2015/04/16/newtown_creek_shows_ signs_of_poop-g.php (accessed March 20, 2019).

3 Jeff Reuben, "Long Before Newtown Creek Became a Superfund Site, an 1881 Crusade Tried to Save It," *Untapped Cities* (April 5, 2016), https://untappedcities.com/2016/04/05/long-before-newtown-creek-became-a-superfund-site-an-1881-crusade-tried-to-save-it/ (Accessed March 23, 2019).

4 *The Newtown Creek Industrial District of New York City* (New York: Merchants' Association Industrial Bureau, 1921), 10–11. https://babel.hathitrust.org/cgi/pt?id=nnc1. cu03357732;view=1up;seq=5, (accessed March 23, 2019).

5 NYC Planning "Manufacturing Districts: M3," https://www1.nyc.gov/site/planning/zoning/ districts-tools/m3.page (accessed March 20, 2019).

6 *Newtown Creek Brownfield Opportunity Area Report* (2012).

7 Riverkeeper, "Greenpoint Oil Spill on Newtown Creek," https://www.riverkeeper.org/ campaigns/stop-polluters/newtown/ (Accessed March 23, 2019).

8 Newtown Creek Community Advisory Group Steering Committee, "Vision Principles for Newtown Creek Restoration & Remediation" (April 2016).

9 Perkins + Will "Newtown Creek Vision Plan," https://perkinswill.com/work/newtown-creek-vision-plan (accessed March 9, 2019).

10 Elizabeth Meyer, "Uncertain Parks: Disturbed Sites, Citizens, and Risk Society," in Julia Czerniak & George Hargreaves (eds), *Large Parks* (New York: Princeton Architectural Press, 2007), 59.

somewhere, and that somewhere is essential to the vitality of the here and now. The Newtown Creek is no longer, and will never again be, the tidal estuary it once was. The only force that advances discharge from CSOs is more discharge from CSOs. A recently proposed $1.4 billion sewage detention system aims to reduce the volume of CSO discharge by about 62% – but this only means that less discharge will enter the creek. Consequentially, it also means greater stagnation and increased aeration.[16]

As designers continue to advocate for the density of cities, we should understand and accept the reciprocal growth and necessary evils of their support landscapes and approach them with honesty, openness, and nuance. The Newtown Creek presents impossible challenges, but within those challenges lays opportunity for creative imagination and innovation. As Marcel Proust wrote, perhaps "the real voyage of discovery consists, not in seeking new landscapes, but in having new eyes."[17] More than just foils for designed, benevolent landscapes, when embraced for their "otherness," toxic support landscapes like the Newtown Creek present rich, odorous, disgusting, paradoxically beautiful, and oft-ignored possibilities for cities now and into the future.

11 Picon, "Anxious Landscapes," 64.

12 Kathleen McAuliffe, "Disgust Made Us Human," *Aeon* (June 6, 2016), https://aeon.co/essays/how-disgust-made-humans-cooperate-to-build-civilisations, (Accessed March 23, 2019).

13 Mary Douglas, *Purity and Danger: An Analysis of Concepts of Pollution and Taboo* (New York: Frederick A. Praeger Publishers, 1966), 2.

14 Carolyn Korsmeyer, *Savoring Disgust: The Foul & The Fair in Aesthetics* (New York: Oxford University Press, 2011), 3.

15 Perkins + Will, the firm that produced the Newtown Creek Vision Plan, also proposed a massive rezoning of the Newtown Creek to accommodate a "Newtown Makerhood." See Perkins + Will, "Making it to 9 Million and Beyond" (February 7, 2017), http://blog.perkinswill.com/making-it-to-9-million-and-beyond/ (accessed March 23, 2019).

16 Letter from Joseph DiMura (director, Bureau of Water Compliance, NY State Department of Environmental Conservation) to Keith Mahoney (acting program manager, Long Term Control Plan, Bureau of Wastewater Treatment, NYC Department of Environmental Protection), June 27, 2018, https://www.dec.ny.gov/docs/water_pdf/62718pprnewtcrltcp.pdf.

17 Marcel Proust, *La Prisionière* (1923).

Above: Industrial infrastructure on the banks of the Newtown Creek.

Jake Boswell is an assistant professor of landscape architecture at The Ohio State University and former Andrew W. Mellon Fellow at Dumbarton Oaks. Boswell's work traces the impact of social and scientific imaginaries on the production of designed and vernacular landscapes with a specific focus on the role of climate. His writings and speculative design work have received recognition in numerous journals and international design competitions including the LA+ IMAGINATION international design ideas competition (2017).

+ ENVIRONMENTAL HUMANITIES, MEDIA STUDIES

A 2008 World Wildlife Fund (WWF) poster campaign featuring the head and torso of a mutant man-fish carries the inscription, "Stop climate change before it changes you." The ad is curious because it seems to suggest that climate change will have a peculiar impact on humanity – our degeneration into a sub-human species. But why? In the 21st century do we honestly believe that an altered climate will somehow produce an altered body? If it did, would that be bad?

While the term "mutant" did not come into common use until Hugo de Vries introduced his theory of evolution by mutation in 1901, fascination with the human body's ability to change, and the conditions under which it might do so have existed for thousands of years. In this paper, I argue that since the late 18th century the idea of the mutant has gone through at least three distinct phases, each of which uses the fictionalized body of the mutant as a foil for contemporaneous techno-social questions and fears. Briefly, I define these phases as the degenerate mutant, the mutant as environmental avenger, and, finally, the mutant as neo-Lamarckian semaphore. Because the western cultural construction of the mutant maps closely to changing anxieties about the human body in relation to its environment, I argue that the image of the mutant is a valuable index for understanding and projecting the evolution of popular environmental discourse. I end with thoughts on what the contemporary image of the mutant may mean for design, and for landscape architecture in particular.

The mutant is a complicated figure in the western imaginary, especially in reference to climate. Questions of human plasticity and its association with changes in climate are old. European encounters with the tropical world from the 15th century onward raised critical questions about the nature of the human body when exposed to different climates. What caused people of different countries to display such variation in color, habit, and temperament? More importantly, could European life be sustained outside of a European climate? Codification of the scientific debate surrounding the question of human plasticity

JAKE BOSWELL

ON HUMAN PLASTICITY

can be traced to the 18th-century naturalists Carolus Linnaeus and George-Louis Leclerc, Comte de Buffon. Linnaeus's 1758 edition of *Systemae Naturae*, proposed five subspecies within the designation *Homo sapiens: africanus, americanus, asiaticus, europeanus, and ferus* (or wild) assigning each particular physical features, customs, and humors.[1] Following Linnaeus, Buffon, in his 1766 essay *"De la Dègènèration des Animaux"* theorized that the various types of humanity were attributable to variations in climate. Buffon suggested that the European racial type was the rootstock from which all other forms of humanity descended, and that other races had emerged over the course of many centuries following their migration to other climates. Such climatic mutations could be reversed, Buffon suggested, by returning degenerate human populations to a European climate.[2] The notion of climate's effect on the body would eventually become folded into Jean-Baptiste Lamarck's theory of evolution, which saw all evolutionary change as inherently driven by characteristics acquired in response to environmental stimuli.

By the middle of the 19th century, scientists sought to use the new and seemingly objective and precise technology of photography to document the process of human degeneration. The historian Nancy Stepan has documented the 1865 photographic expedition organized and led by American biologist Louis Agassiz to Brazil in order to document what Agassiz supposed to be the degenerate bodies of the mulatto and mestizo populations.[3] Such studies eventually co-informed the rise of eugenics policies in the US and Europe at the end of the 19th century. Notably, Agassiz's study prefigures that of Francis Galton (whose use of photography for the identification of criminal types provided the quasi-scientific underpinnings for the eugenics movement) by more than a decade.

Given the horror with which eugenics played out in Nazi Germany and, to a lesser degree, other western nations (including the US) it is not surprising that post-war Western society dropped all pretense to its desirability. And yet, the WWF's anti-climate change man-fish participates, albeit unwittingly, in many of the same essentializing tropes that informed and animated the eugenics movement. Here is the image of a human that has seemingly degenerated in the face of a warmer, ostensibly wetter, climate.

While the degenerate mutant appears in literature throughout the 19th century, it was widely popularized via the unabashed eugenicist H.G. Wells. The half man, half animal, mutants inhabiting *The Island of Dr. Moreau*, emerge from Wells's study of Mendelian genetics.[4] A prominent biologist in his day, Wells used fiction as a way to explore the emergence of Weismannism and the final collapse of Lamarckian theories on the inheritance of acquired characteristics.[5] For mutants, Wells is a bridge figure, straddling the 19th and 20th centuries and the realms of high culture, scientific inquiry, and the popular mass media. Pulp series like Edgar Rice Burroughs's *Tarzan* and Arthur Conan Doyle's *Professor Challenger* that emerged following the

success of Wells's novels, took the often pathetically degenerate tropical mutant and transformed it into the savage antagonist of countless jingoistic adventure stories. Savage mutants of the Burroughs variety remained a consistent figure in pulp fiction and comics until after WWII when a new generation of writers would recast them.

The first manifestation of the post-war, post-eugenics, mutant surfaced in A.E. van Vogt's 1946 novel *Slan*, in which a psychic race of genetically modified humans called Slans, are hunted to near extinction by humans who fear the arrival of a superior species. Similarly, in John Wyndham's the *Crysalids* (1955), a group of mutant children, also psychics, attempt to escape extermination by a morally and genetically repressive society in a now sub-tropical, post-nuclear holocaust Labrador. Importantly, both of these novels feature mutants as marginalized, persecuted communities who use their mutant powers as a way to confound or escape further persecution. This feature of the post-war mutant has led many theorists to argue that, following the Holocaust, the post-war mutant is an allegorical stand-in for Jews.[6] This allegory is particularly noticeable in comics. Stan Lee and Jack Kirby introduced the *X-Men* in 1964, introducing the world to what would emerge as a common 20th-century trope, a persecuted or shunned community of mutants who use their powers for good.

However, if this post-war mutant can be read as an allegory of otherness, it can also be read as a reaction to humanity's dawning concern for the effects of technology on the environment. Lawrence Buell and, later, Ursula Heise, identified a late 20th-century socio-technical imaginary, which they call "toxic discourse."[7] Toxic discourse is, to quote Buell, "expressed anxiety arising from the perceived threat of environmental hazard due to chemical modification by human agency."[8] As Buell and Heise point out, the most important thing to emerge from toxic discourse is undoubtedly the environmental movement and, subsequently, the environmentally conscious citizen, beginning with Rachel Carson's *Silent Spring* in 1962. I would argue that its second most important product is a reconceptualization of its sometimes-central protagonist, the mutant.

In the wake of major toxic events like Love Canal, Three Mile Island, and even Rachel Carson's own very public battle with cancer, a new type of mutant hero emerges. In comics like Stan Lee's *Spiderman* (1962), *The Hulk* (1962), and *Daredevil* (1964), Len Wein's *Swamp Thing* (1971), Kevin Eastman and Peter Laird's *Teenage Mutant Ninja Turtles* (1984), or films like Michael Hertz and Lloyd Kaufman's *The Toxic Avenger* (1984), mutants are created through direct contact with a toxic substance. Spiderman is bitten by a radioactive spider; Daredevil and the Teenage Mutant Ninja Turtles are struck by the same bouncing canister of toxic "mutagen." Such toxic creations often go on to battle the corporate forces of pollution (and ninjas) that created them – what Ulrich Beck has referred to as the Shadow Kingdom, a corporate, industrial malevolence, which, in Beck's interpretation, is "hidden behind the visible

world and threatens human life on this Earth."⁹ Far from the pathetic tropical degeneracy of the 19th century or even the signification of repressed otherness of the immediate post-war, the late 20th-century mutant–often an unintended byproduct of the Shadow Kingdom–emerges as humanity's champion – doing battle with the uncertain, unseen, and unknowable forces of toxicity antithetical to human existence.

While certainly less point-source than a radioactive spider or vat of toxic ooze, climate change easily falls within the same vein of environmental uncertainty. Indeed, long before the WWF poster campaign, a progenitor of our man-fish had already surfaced amidst the crowd of sci-fi mutants. The failed 1995 movie *Waterworld* featured a gilled and web-footed Kevin Costner as "The Mariner" – a mutant adapted for life within an emphatically more oceanic post-climate change world, and its reluctant savior. Yet our 2008 man-fish is a decidedly more ambivalent figure, straddling 19th-century tropical fears while still forwarding a rather pathetic hope for genetic perseverance in the face of a rapidly shifting planet. Perhaps this ambivalence is a symptom of the seemingly intractable nature of climate change and the slowly eroding ability to alter or reverse our planetary fortunes. Just as the degenerate mutant of the 19th century was a product of the uncontrollable force of a region's climate on the body, the contemporary neo-Lamarckian mutant embodied in the WWF ad is a response to our uncertainty about controlling our climatic future. As such, this new mutant would persist even in the face of a radical environmental shift, its body becoming an index of the change itself. Other more recent mutants reinforce this argument, the Craker's and Pigoons of Margaret Atwood's acclaimed *MaddAddam* trilogy (2003–2013), the New People of Paulo Bacigalupi's *The Windup Girl* (2009), and the genetically engineered soldiers of Netflix's *The Titan* (2018) may be better adapted for survival in an altered world (or off-world in the case of *The Titan*), but none are equipped for (or even interested in) doing battle with the forces that are changing it.

In 2008 Ursula Heise introduced the term "eco-cosmopolitanism" as a response to what she sees as the failure of contemporary environmentalism to address global environmental issues while acknowledging non-western and non-human perspective. Eco-cosmopolitanism, borrows cosmopolitanism's "cultural and political understanding that allows individuals to think beyond the boundaries of their own cultures, ethnicities, or nations to a range of other sociocultural frameworks" while reaching toward a post-human appreciation for the perspective of nonhuman species and rejecting traditional environmentalism's reliance on localism and pastoral notions of steady-state ecological systems.¹⁰ If, as Heise argues, eco-cosmopolitanism is our path toward imagining a non-zero sum environmental future, then the mutant–an allegory for the marginalized and persecuted, whose body shifts and adapts to an uncertain environment–would seem to be the 21st century's ideal eco-cosmopolitan citizen. This theory is borne out by the staggering number of mutant oriented summer blockbusters over the last decade as well as the number and variety of DIY body hacking and at-home CRISPR kits available for purchase on the web.

But is this a cop-out? The projection of consumerism's underbelly onto the pop-culture manifestation of Beck's Shadow Kingdom allowed mass culture to "battle" the forces of toxicity without challenging the consumerist impulse that underwrites it. Similarly, the ability to intentionally alter our bodies in response to the environment would seem to absolve humanity of its responsibility for climate change in the first place. The idea that we can adapt our bodies to accommodate an increasingly hostile environment without the need to change our patterns of waste and consumption–and perhaps even as a product of that consumption–is a dangerous one.

What, then, is the way forward? The presence of this article in a design journal should raise questions about design's, and particularly landscape architecture's role in responding to–and perhaps helping to shape–popular discourse on climate

1 Carl von Linné, *A General System of Nature, Through the Three Grand Kingdoms of Animals, Vegetables, and Minerals, Systematically Divided into Their Several Classes, Orders, Genera, Species, and Varieties, With Their Habitations, Manners, Economy, Structure, and Peculiarities*, trans. William Turton (London: Lackington, Allen & Company, 1802), 9.

2 Benjamin Isaac, *The Invention of Racism in Classical Antiquity* (Princeton, NJ: Princeton University Press, 2004), 9.

3 Nancy Stepan, *Picturing Tropical Nature* (London: Reaktion Books Ltd., 2001), 85–119.

4 If you're a comic book fan you probably realize that I'm conflating two communities. For the uninitiated, the Marvel universe makes a distinction between two varieties of mutant: mutants and mutates. In essence, a mutant is born (e.g., Wolverine, Cyclops, Jean Grey, ostensibly our man-fish), while a mutate is made (e.g., Spiderman, Swamp Thing, the Teenage Mutant Ninja Turtles).

5 Weismannism is the forerunner of the evolutionary concept of descent with variation through genetic mutation; that is, that species change through a slow process of random variation and natural selection, rather than changing quickly in response to their environment. Most famously, August Weismann (to finally discredit Lamarkianism), cut the tails from 901 white mice over five generations to show that, no matter how many generations of mice had tails surgically removed, new generations would still have tails. For a good discussion of this in the context of Wells's writing see Leon Stover, "Editor's Introduction" in H.G Wells & Leon Stover, *The Island of Dr. Moreau: A Critical Text of the 1896 London First Edition, With an Introduction and Appendices* (Jefferson, NC: MacFarland & Company, 1996), 1.

6 See for instance, Simcha Weinstein, *Up, Up, and Oy Vey!: How Jewish History, Culture, and Values Shaped the Comic Book Superhero* (Baltimore: Leviathan Press, 2006); or Danny Fingeroth, Disguised as Clark Kent: Jews, Comics, and the Creation of the Superhero (New York: Continuum, 2007).

7 Lawrence Buell, "Toxic Discourse" *Critical Inquiry* 24 (1998): 639–65; Ursula K. Heise, *Sense of Place and Sense of Planet: the Environmental Imagination of the Global* (Oxford: Oxford University Press, 2008), 160–77.

8 Lawrence Buell, *Writing for an Endangered World: Literature, Culture, and Environment in the U.S. and Beyond* (Cambridge, Mass: Belknap Press of Harvard University Press, 2001), 31.

9 Ulrich Beck & Mark Ritter, *Risk Society: Towards a New Modernity* (London: Sage Publications, 1992), 72.

10 Ibid, 60–65; or see Ursula Heise, "How We Became Aliens" *LA+ Interdisciplinary Journal of Landscape Architecture* 5 (2017): 10–17.

11 Elizabeth K. Meyer, "Uncertain Parks: Disturbed Sites, Citizens, and Risk Society," in Julia Czerniak & George Hargreaves (eds), *Large Parks* (New York: Princeton Architectural Press, 2007), 75.

change and our adaptation to it. To be clear, I am not suggesting that mutants are an appropriate metaphor for landscapes. Landscapes are not mutants in this sense regardless of their programmatic or ecological hybridity. Landscape mutantism is not my aim. But, like the body of the mutant, landscapes can be cultural indices of change. Landscapes, therefore, can serve as powerful haptic tools for recording and clarifying that change to make it legible. In her 2007 essay "Uncertain Parks," Elizabeth Meyer makes this point in reference to large parks built on former sites of waste and toxicity. Meyer argues, "If our collective identity has been shaped by our shared patterns of consumption, and those patterns have led to unintended environmental degradation, the reuse of degraded sites as parks might resurrect the park's agency as a vehicle for engendering new connections between private actions and public values, between individuals and the world."[11]

Meyer's point is that fixing these sites isn't enough, but that such sites should also act as a way to confront our complicity in the site's creation. Similarly, when designing sites impacted by climate change (eventually all sites, theoretically), I would argue that it isn't enough to fix the immediate problem if we don't also ask the people who use or benefit from those sites to see, engage with, and recognize their role in that change. Fortunately, like the "peculiar beauty" that Meyer observes in sites of waste and toxicity, climate change has aesthetic ramifications and possibilities as well. Changing patterns of temperature, precipitation, and phenology have already begun to precipitate changes in the everyday built environment of our cities and regions. As these changes occur, landscape architects should use them. Plant hardiness zones will shift, microclimates will become increasingly apparent and increasingly useful, water will become more plentiful in some regions and less plentiful in others, and its periodicity will change. All of these are opportunities for landscape architects to reveal.

If we learn anything from the 19th-century degenerate mutant or the 20th-century mutant avenger, it's that the limits of human plasticity within the bounds of contemporary science are pretty narrow. Our bodies don't change – at least not fast enough to turn us into fish-people in time to keep us from drowning. What we can change are our habits – especially if we're confronted with their consequences.

VITAL CONNECTIONS
DESIGNING ECOLOGICAL NETWORKS

ANDREW GONZALEZ

Andrew Gonzalez is professor and Liber Ero Chair in Biodiversity Conservation in the Department of Biology, McGill University. He is the founding director of the Quebec Centre for Biodiversity Science. His research is focused on the causes and consequences of biodiversity change and the application of biodiversity science to restore ecosystems and the many benefits they provide society. In 2017, he spoke at the World Economic Forum in Davos on the sixth mass extinction and designing resilient ecosystems for urban sustainability.

✚ ECOLOGY, ENVIRONMENTAL SCIENCE

One of the great societal challenges of this century is to manage the risks to human well-being arising from biodiversity change and ecosystem degradation. These risks are increasing because of the tightening feedbacks between human and ecological systems from local to global scales.[1] In this article, I develop the idea that network science can be applied to understand and mitigate these risks by restoring ecological connectivity and thereby the sustainability of human transformed landscapes.[2]

Sustainability science focuses on understanding the interactions, both direct and indirect, between the structure and functioning of ecosystems and the human activities that affect their production of ecosystem services in the long term. Sustainability results from a dynamic balance between natural degrading processes and human disturbances on the one hand, and regenerative natural processes and protective human management on the other.[3] Locally, for example, this can mean compensating for the ecological and economic impacts of tree mortality due to infestation of urban forests by an exotic insect pest,[4] or regionally the sustainability of multiple interconnected fisheries affected by decadal climate fluctuations, and globally assessing the long-term yield of the world's crops given changing climate extremes and improved technologies. As we move up these scales we encompass a broader array of connected social and ecological feedbacks within which sustainability can be framed as a network problem.

Framed as a network problem ecological sustainability is about how the long-term persistence of ecosystems depends upon the presence of ever-changing flows of information, energy and resources among the ecosystem nodes in the network. As I discuss below, we now understand that these flows mediate levels of biodiversity and the supply of ecosystem services. In ecosystem networks, fluctuations arise in response to unpredictable variation in the environment (e.g., climate extremes) and the inherent dynamics of ecological and evolutionary process. In this fluctuation-view of the natural world, sustainability is always bounded in time and space, and what we choose to sustain must be assessed and managed at multiple spatial and temporal scales.[5]

An ecosystem is sustainable relative to fluctuations occurring over a certain range of changing conditions to which its component species are adapted (e.g., annual or decadal climate variability). Ecologists have found that spatial connectivity, in the form of the flows described above, allow the dynamic persistence of genetic and species diversity and this translates into sustained flows of ecosystem processes and dampened fluctuations across the network.[6] Evolutionary dynamics are also a vital part of ecological sustainability, because patterns of natural selection may allow species to adapt, sometimes rapidly, to changing environmental conditions. Here genetic diversity and rates of diversification define the evolutionary potential of the system, but also determine which ecosystem services will persist in the long term.

The long-held view that evolution is a slow process is being upturned; ecological and evolutionary processes are now understood to interact, resulting in eco-evolutionary feedbacks, which affect the degree to which the system can respond and adapt to environmental change.[7]

Ecological Networks in Theory

Pressed by the severity and scale of the problem of habitat loss and fragmentation,[8] conservation science has developed the science and policy support (an IUCN connectivity conservation specialist group) for implementing spatial ecological networks as an integrated conservation strategy.[9] A spatial ecological network (SEN) is defined as a system of ecosystem elements, or patches, that are configured and managed with the objective of maintaining, or restoring, ecological connectivity as a means of conserving biodiversity and ecosystem functioning and services.[10] This approach to landscape conservation integrates people and aims to understand the feedbacks between the social and the ecological process occurring within the SEN. The application of SEN in human transformed land and seascapes involves methods from network science and decision theory to identify functionally connected networks.[11] The aim of SENs has been to meet multiple criteria, such as maximizing the persistence of a set of target species, for a given investment in area allocated to the SEN. Recently the stated goals of SEN have been broadened to social-ecological criteria that include the sustainability of ecosystem services and their resilience to environmental change.[12]

However, this approach is not without its critics.[13] Concern has been raised about overly simplistic landscape planning where connectivity is applied as a rule.[14] This criticism is often relevant because: 1) links in the SEN defining connectivity are taken as fixed in space and time, even though many species show variable patterns of movement, and 2) monitoring is not in place to assess the SEN's state as the connectivity changes, or as new demands are placed on it through human resource exploitation. Without these measures, it is impossible to establish whether a proposed SEN is the right option in the long term given available investment and anticipated risks.[15] The next generation of SEN models and planning must assess, model, and manage the feedbacks between the network's structure and dynamics and how these influence adaptation to perturbations within the network.

Let's make the notion of a spatial ecological network more precise. An SEN is composed of nodes (or vertices) and links, where the nodes represent individual ecological entities (e.g., a patch of habitat or ecosystem type) and the edges represent connections or flows between the nodes (e.g., via active or passive movement), which are often weighted, directional, and fluctuating in strength.[16] Methods for network planning are now built on a powerful array of tools for identifying the nodes and links of an SEN, and for ranking the importance of these nodes and links to the network's structure, such as connectivity at multiple scales.[17] In many cases, the configuration of the network's nodes and links are considered static, where nodes and links defining connectivity are fixed and unchanging through time.[18] But although this representation might be valid in the short term, this is unlikely to be true over the long term. The importance of nodes and links varies through time because of fluctuations in the biological and physical environment. A clear example is the time and space varying connectivity of a river network during alternating periods of flooding and drought. Organisms occupying these networks will experience a highly dynamic habitat. Another example is range expansion by a population under climate change, where individuals move across entire regions to track shifting environmental conditions.[19] Plans for SENs rarely use models of the dynamics (gain and loss) of the network's node and link structure, even though these may be far from steady-state due to large-scale factors, such as climate change.

An SEN is also dynamic because the ecological and evolutionary states of its nodes (e.g., population abundances, species, or genetic diversity) change over time. Nodes change state over time because the dynamics depend not only on past states, but also on the state of the nodes with which it is interacting and the flow of information through the links connecting them. Predicting the dynamics of the network's nodes from the flows of information through the network's topology is very challenging. However, recently significant progress has been made, and it is now possible to explore the interplay between network topology and dynamics and even to separate the contribution of topology and dynamics to the network's response to perturbations and its resilience to them.[20] In principle, an SEN's spatial structure could be designed to protect and manage the flows mediating the levels of biodiversity and ecosystem functioning. In most instances, however, we do not possess quantitative estimates of species' movements in conjunction with the flows of energy, resources, and information across an SEN. Dynamic models of SEN are data hungry, and the datasets required are costly to assemble because they involve monitoring, both on the ground and by earth observation systems. But, if we are to manage an SEN for time and space varying risks, we need to understand how changes to the network's configuration affects its dynamics and vice versa.[21] We must understand which features of the network's configuration can be managed to maintain desirable system properties (e.g., biodiversity, adaptive capacity, ecosystem functioning) within trajectories that are kept away from irreversible degradation or collapse. This focus links SEN design to the burgeoning theory of network robustness and the idea that an SEN's configuration can be managed to maintain biodiversity and ecosystem services within a range of ecological and socially desirable conditions.

Ecological Networks in Practice

In 2009, I received a request from the Ministry of Sustainable Development, Environment, and Parks of the Quebec government to identify a habitat network for the long-term conservation of forests and their associated animal biodiversity for the region surrounding the city of Montreal in southern Quebec, Canada. Extending from the Appalachian Mountains in the southeast to the Laurentian Mountains in the northwest, the study area of 27,500 km2 encompasses ~40% forest, which in many parts is heavily fragmented due to the predominance of productive agroecosystems in the St. Lawrence lowlands. Ongoing urban sprawl to the north and south of the city is altering forest patch area, degrees of fragmentation, shape, quality, and connectivity. Projections of future forest loss and scenarios of likely climate change, derived from regional climate models, make the conservation of ecological connectivity an imperative for this region in the coming years.

Three aspects are crucial to the effective design of habitat networks. First, they must meet the distinct habitat requirements of a wide array of species throughout their life cycles. Second, habitat networks must accommodate different movement types, including short-range connectivity relevant to the persistence of populations within the forest network and long-range connectivity relevant to climate-driven range shifts across the region. Third, the forest network must be robust to future forest loss and changing climate. Future land-use and climate change scenarios are uncertain, so network design should allow for the broadest range of future conditions.

We adopted a multicriteria spatial optimization approach to the design of a habitat network. Our methodology produced a spatial prioritization of forest ecosystems that maintained connectivity across the network. Multi-criteria decision methods and sustained stakeholder engagement were essential for the SEN approach to be adopted for conservation.[22] Broad engagement with stakeholders helped balance the various social, economic, and ecological needs in the region especially where resources for land protection are scarce.[23] Our analysis identified the habitat networks that best met the short- and long-distance movements and the contrasting habitat needs of 14 vertebrate species. The nodes in the network were prioritized for their quality as habitat for these species and their contribution to the connectivity of the SEN. In the second step we compared the current day connectivity of the landscape with projections of how it will change in the future depending on the percentage of the forest that is protected. This was done using different scenarios of land use and climate change projected by computer models. We compared a business-as-usual scenario with three conservation scenarios in which 5%, 10%, or 17% of the area was protected for connectivity.

With the 17% scenario, the negative effects of land-use change on connectivity were much reduced relative to our other scenarios, especially the business-as-usual scenario. Moreover, this 17% scenario led to a greater retention of the different conservation criteria: including habitat quality, connectivity, and suitability for adaptation to climate change. This research has guided decision-making and ecosystem restoration. Over time the SEN will be protected and expanded through the addition of protected nodes (via forest planting and restoration) and links (forest corridors).

1 D. Moran & K. Kanemoto, "Identifying Species Threat Hotspots from Global Supply Chains," *Nature Ecology & Evolution* 1 (2017): doi:10.1038/s41559-016-0023.

2 L. Boitani, et al., "Ecological Networks as Conceptual Frameworks or Operational Tools in Conservation," *Conservation Biology* 21 (2007): 1414–22; A. Gonzalez, P. Thompson & M. Loreau, "Spatial Ecological Networks: Planning for Sustainability in the Long Term," *Current Opinion in Environmental Sustainability* 29 (2018): 187–97.

3 J. Norberg & G. Cumming, *Complexity Theory for a Sustainable Future* (New York: Columbia University Press, 2008).

4 For example, the case of the Emerald Ash Borer.

5 F. Isbell, et al., "Linking the Influence and Dependence of People and Biodiversity Across Scales," *Nature* 546 (2017): 65–71.

6 P.L. Thompson, B. Rayfield & A. Gonzalez, "Loss of Habitat and Connectivity Erodes Species Diversity, Ecosystem Functioning and Stability in Metacommunity Networks," *Ecography* (2016): doi: 10.1111/ecog.02558.

7 A. Gonzalez, et al., "Evolutionary Rescue: An Emerging Focus at the Intersection between Ecology and Evolution," *Philosophical Transactions of the Royal Society B: Biological Sciences* 368 (2013): doi: 10.1098/rtsb.2012.0404.

8 N.M. Haddad, et al., "Habitat Fragmentation and its Lasting Impact on Earth's Ecosystems," *Science Advances* 1 (2015): e1500052.

9 K.R. Crooks & M. Sanjayan, *Connectivity Conservation* (Cambridge: Cambridge University Press, 2006); S.J. Leroux, et al., "Minimum Dynamic Reserves: A Framework for Determining Reserve Size in Ecosystems Structured by Large Disturbances," *Biolgical Conservation* 138 (2007): 464–73.

10 Modified from G. Bennett, "Integrating Biodiversity Conservation and Sustainable Use: Lessons Learned From Ecological Networks" (International Union for Conservation of Nature and Natural Resources, 2014).

11 Crooks & Sanjayan, *Connectivity Conservation*, ibid; Leroux, "Minimum Dynamic Reserves," ibid.

12 See, e.g., Bennett, "Integrating Biodiversity Conservation and Sustainable Use," ibid; G.S. Cumming, "The Relevance and Resilience of Protected Areas in the Anthropocene," *Anthropocene* 13 (2016): 46–56.

13 S. Gippoliti & C. Battisti, "More Cool than Tool: Equivoques, Conceptual Traps and Weakness of Ecological Networks in Environmental Planning and Conservation," *Land Use Policy* 68 (2017): 686–91.

14 Ibid.

15 Ibid.

16 M.R.T. Dale & M.J. Fortin, "From Graphs to Spatial Graphs," *Annual Review of Ecology & Systematics* 41 (2010): 21–38.

17 Ibid.; T.E. Dilts, et al., "Multiscale Connectivity and Graph Theory Highlight Critical Areas for Conservation Under Climate Change," *Ecological Applications* 26 (2016): 1223–37; A. Moilanen, "On the Limitations of Graph-theoretic Connectivity in Spatial Ecology and Conservation," *Journal of Applied Ecology* 48 (2011): 1543–47.

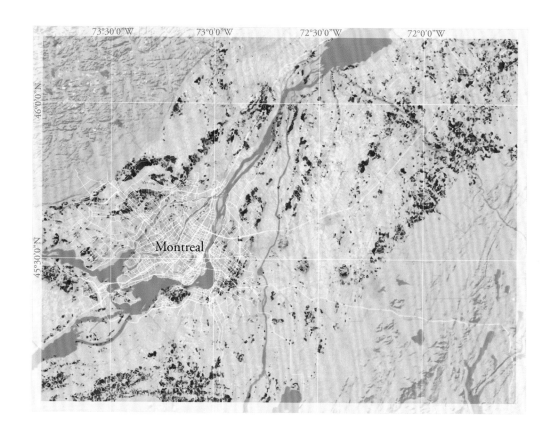

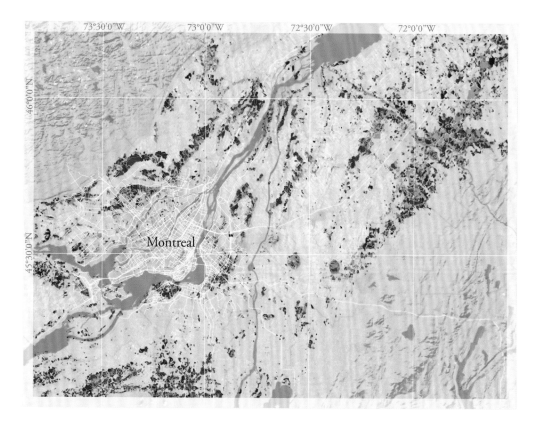

We showed that accounting for connectivity in spatial prioritization strongly modifies conservation priorities. I recommend the use of realistic scenario-based projections of climate and land-use change so as to future-proof the structure of the SEN being protected. Given the investment required to acquire, restore, and protect ecosystems within a network, it is important for the network's connectivity to be robust to as many likely scenarios of change as possible. Although experiments at the landscape scale are impractical, scenario simulations can be used to capture the range of impacts of future fragmentation on biodiversity and explore how regional network planning will interact with regional development to modify SEN connectivity and robustness to disturbances. The identification of an SEN for Montreal was founded on a sustained, multi-year engagement with regional stakeholders[24] (including governments at several scales and NGOs) that had broadly discussed scenarios of environmental risk and addressed different options for managing connectivity for biodiversity and ecosystem services. The medium-term goal is the protection of an SEN for the entire St. Lawrence Lowlands. Our approach to the design of the SEN for the region around Montreal, is now part of a multi-stakeholder effort to implement a greenbelt for the city.

The Anthropocene is characterized by changes in the connectivity of social and ecological systems at all spatial scales. The multiscale nature of changing connectivity is creating outcomes with impacts large enough to threaten local and regional biodiversity and the long-term sustainability of the ecosystem processes, and benefits we obtain from them. Earlier, I stressed the importance of understanding the feedbacks between the network structure of SENs and the ecological dynamics that together define robustness and sustainability of the network's properties. SEN identification and prioritization based on multiscale and multi-criteria connectivity analyses have great potential to inform land planning for long-term sustainability. The co-design of an SEN with a diverse array of actors and stakeholders is an essential part of establishing the trust and cooperation needed for its social acceptability across different sectors of society, and the polycentric modes of governance that are needed to adaptively monitor SEN and manage them in the long term.

18 See, e.g., Crooks & Sanjayan, *Connectivity Conservation*, ibid; Boitani, et al., "Ecological Networks as Conceptual Frameworks," ibid; Gippoliti & Battisti: "More Cool than Tool," ibid.

19 E.R. Fronhofer, N. Nitsche & F. Altermatt, "Information Use Shapes the Dynamics of Range Expansions into Environmental Gradients," *Global Ecology & Biogeography* 26 (2017): 400–11.

20 B. Barzel & A-L. Barabasi, "Universality in Network Dynamics," *Nature Physics* 9 (2013): 673–81; U. Harush & B. Barzel, "Dynamic Patterns of Information Flow in Complex Networks," *Nature Communications* 8 (2017): 2181; M. Barbier, et al., "Generic Assembly Patterns in Complex Ecological Communities," *Proceedings of the National Academy of Sciences USA* (2018).

21 Ibid.

22 I.B. Huang, J. Keisler & Linkov, "Multi-criteria Decision Analysis in Environmental Sciences: Ten Years of Applications and Trends," *Science of the Total Environment* 409 (2011): 3578–94.

23 Ibid; A. Moilanen, J.R. Leathwick & J.M. Quinn, "Spatial Prioritization of Conservation Management," *Conservation Letters* 4 (2011): 383–93; M. Convertino & J.L. Valverde, "Portfolio Decision Analysis Framework for Value-focused Ecosystem Management," *PLoS One* 8 (2013): e65056.

24 M. Mitchell, et al., "The Montérégie Connection: Linking Landscapes, Biodiversity, and Ecosystem Services to Improve Decision Making," *Ecology & Society* 20 (2015): 15.

Acknowledgments: The author was supported in this research by an NSERC Discovery grant, a Killam Fellowship, and the Liber Ero Chair in Biodiversity Conservation. The author acknowledges collaborations with Dr Cecile Albert, Dr Bronwyn Rayfield, Maria Dumitru, Dr Patrick Thompson, and Professor Michel Loreau.

Left: At top, a map of the Montreal study area showing good quality habitat suitable for the conservation of biodiversity; below, the habitat network now including habitat connectivity as a criterion for conservation.

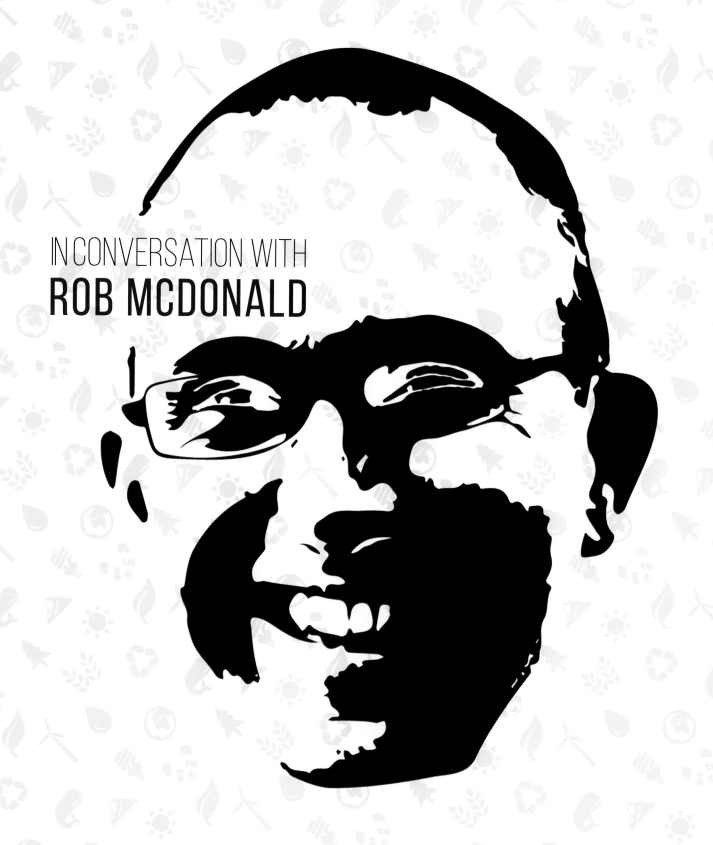

IN CONVERSATION WITH
ROB MCDONALD

Rob McDonald is lead scientist for Global Cities at The Nature Conservancy. He has been writing and researching about the challenges of conservation in an era of rapid urbanization and climate change for more than a decade, producing more than 50 peer-reviewed publications and a recent book entitled *Conservation for Cities* (2015). Prior to joining The Nature Conservancy, he was a Smith Conservation Biology Fellow at Harvard, where he taught landscape ecology courses in the GSD. **Richard Weller** and **Billy Fleming** spoke with Rob about the evolution of the conservation movement, the unique challenges posed by climate change, and the Conservancy's vision for the future of the planet.

+ How does The Nature Conservancy work?

The Nature Conservancy is a global environmental non-profit, with headquarters in Arlington, Virginia. We have a global board that directs our actions, including choosing who will be our CEO. We have about one million members, primarily but not exclusively located in the United States, whose donations supply the majority of our funding.

Operationally, within the Conservancy there are geographical offices that direct work in a specific state or country. These field offices are still the hub of much of our on-the-ground conservation activity. There are also strategy teams that work globally on a specific issue. I am lead scientist on the Cities team within the Conservancy, one of our global strategy teams. We focus on the benefits that nature in and near cities can supply for human well-being and biodiversity. We have roughly 80 cities globally where the Conservancy has a project. Often, these involve bringing information on the value of nature into urban planning processes.

+ The conservation movement has evolved from local activism in the mid-20th century to now have international geopolitical and economic influence. Where does the The Nature Conservancy fit into this recent history?

The Nature Conservancy was founded more than 60 years ago by ecologists in the Ecological Society of America who wanted to form a group that would actively try to conserve nature. Because of that history, the Conservancy has always been science-based and nonpartisan. Our early history concerned local chapters that bought nearby land in order to protect it. While we still do a lot of that work, we now also work on national and international policy where it is important for our mission. There is a shared vision—however broad and perhaps varied—among our members for a greener, sustainable future. That can sound idealistic, and it is. But in order to work happily at an NGO you have to believe in, and fight for, the mission.

The classic division in the environmental movement, formulated perhaps most famously in Roderick Nash's *Wilderness and the American Mind*, is between conservation and preservation. Conservation was focused on wisely using natural resources for future generations, and gave birth to institutions like the US Forest Service and The Nature Conservancy. Preservation was focused on protecting natural areas from human influence, and gave rise to institutions like the US National Parks and The Sierra Club. This division is, I think, a little less clear than it once was. In most practical environmental decisions, one can aim to protect biodiversity and natural areas while also safeguarding human well-being. Groups coming from both traditions often work together.

Another division within the environmental movement is about tactics. Organizations with broad memberships, like The Nature Conservancy, tend to look for solutions to problems that are, when possible, nonconfrontational and consensus-based. On the other extreme are organizations that think it is more successful to call out what they see as bad behavior by corporations and governments. In practice, though, groups at different ends of this spectrum of tactics still find ways to collaborate and work together. I believe both kinds of groups are needed.

+ What kind of nature is The Nature Conservancy trying to conserve?

The Nature Conservancy's mission is to protect the land and waters on which all life depends. So that includes habitat for biodiversity, but also people as well. We see nature conservation as essential for biodiversity and for human well-being. Of course, "nature" is a word with many multifaceted, overlapping meanings. I think it is helpful to think about a gradient of naturalness, from very natural (e.g., a wilderness area) to somewhat natural (e.g., critical natural habitat, their ecosystem processes undoubtedly affected in many ways by nearby urban areas) to a little natural (e.g., green infrastructure such as a constructed wetland). When you think carefully about this gradient, you can see how different actions by conservationists along this spectrum make sense. So conservation groups, including TNC, fight to protect the few wilderness areas left from human influence. We also work, at the same time, to maximize the use of features like constructed wetlands to manage stormwater, rather than concrete pipes. This latter work, in cities, certainly involves designing nature, in the sense of choosing what natural features are where.

+ The Convention on Biological Diversity's deadline for reaching the Aichi targets of securing 17% protected land area and 10% marine area globally is 2020. It is also the end of the UN's decade of thematic emphasis on biodiversity. What's next, or what should be next, in terms of policy and coordination of the global effort to protect biodiversity?

There is a very active debate within the Convention of Biological Diversity (CBD) and the broader conservation community about exactly what comes next. On some metrics, like spurring the creation of protected areas, the CBD has been quite effective. But there are other new threats to biodiversity that haven't been fully dealt with, like climate change. There are some people who want to push for big, visionary goals after 2020 – to have a moment for biodiversity analogous to what the Paris Accords were for the fight against climate change. There are other people who want to focus on protecting and strengthening the gains that have already been made under the CBD rather than pushing for expansive new targets. As an urban ecologist, I have been focused on trying to define what it means to do conservation in the urban century. We are witnessing the greatest migration in human history—this migration of people into cities—and it will have profound implications for how our global economy and society works.

+ It's often said that cities were once perceived as the problem and that now they are a necessary part of the solution. How is The Nature Conservancy working in and with cities?

Our philosophy is to try to minimize the bad from cities, and maximize the good. That is, we promote cities that are resource- and energy-efficient and walkable, as part of a way to make cities more sustainable. I view this as maximizing the positive environmental benefits of urbanization. And we want to have natural features (parks, street trees, rain gardens, etc.) scattered throughout cities, to increase human well-being. On the flip side, we also want to protect critical natural habitat near cities, for the sake of biodiversity. So there is a certain facet of our work in cities, on open space planning, that is focused on minimizing any harms to the environment from urban growth.

+ You have recently published a white paper titled *Nature in the Urban Century: A Global Assessment of Important Areas for Safeguarding Biodiversity and Human Well-being.* The urban growth forecasts it sets out are staggering and your argument is that urban growth can be planned to minimize habitat loss. Can you outline how such planning can take place?

We found, first of all, that urban growth could, if poorly planned, have huge impacts on terrestrial biodiversity. The report shows that urban growth has been responsible for 190,000 km2 of natural habitat loss from 1992 to 2000, 16% of all the natural habitat loss over this period. In the future, this trend will accelerate, especially in tropical moist forests, and potentially urban growth could threaten 290,000 km2 of natural habitat by 2030. However, that future is not written in stone. One of the solutions we describe in the report is urban "greenprinting," planning how natural habitats or natural features (e.g., street trees, public parks, open space, constructed wetlands) can be protected, restored, or created to maximally protect biodiversity and enhance human well-being. Many cities are already trying to do that – there are at least 123 cities globally that have a biodiversity plan or report.

+ Water is often the link between the health of urban and natural systems. How does the competition for water resources impact the vitality of cities and ecosystems?

We are living in a world of increasingly scarce water, and there are many real world examples of competition for water between cities, agriculture, and natural ecosystems in water-scarce areas. However, we try to emphasize in our work the efficient use of water. In many cities, for instance, a substantial fraction of water is lost due to leaky pipes, and if cities can fix that problem then they may be able to withdraw less water from the natural ecosystem.

+ How will this situation be complicated by climate change?

Climate change has several effects on the water cycle. First, since it will be consistently hotter in most places of the world, evaporation and transpiration of water will significantly increase. That leaves rivers less full, all else being equal. It also means that irrigated agriculture will, in many case, need to apply more water. The effects of climate change on precipitation are more complex. In some areas there will be systematic increases in precipitation, in others decreases. One fairly clear trend is a tendency for precipitation to become flashier, so peak rain events may contain more water, and the dry periods in between may be even drier. This has important implications for how cities manage stormwater and flooding risk.

There are of course lots of other impacts of climate change on cities, including sea level rise, and the increased frequency and intensity of heat waves. Cities are having to plan for these myriad impacts all at once, which is quite a challenge!

+ You studied under Richard Forman and are familiar with how designers work. From your perspective, what do most designers get right about vitality in urban and natural systems? Where do they fall short?

My time in the landscape architecture department at the GSD was a very formative time in my career, as it gave me a good sense of how landscape architects and planners approach their task. I see a lot of exciting work incorporating nature into buildings (architecture), projects (landscape architecture), and whole cities (urban planning). The challenge right now for designers in these fields is that there are multiple pathways by which nature benefits people, all of which would necessitate their own design approach if you were to optimize one of them. However, successful plans think about multiple pathways—as well as a whole set of other issues, of course—that you have to consider in successful design. I guess my observation is that sometimes designers approach "putting nature into their plans" from a very simplistic perspective, only thinking about one particular facet of nature. This can sometimes lead to unbalanced and unsuccessful designs.

+ The most optimistic rhetoric coming, for example, from organizations such as the Breakthrough Institute, is that humanity is rational and technology can deliver us to a "good Anthropocene." What do you think?

I think of myself as a pessimistic realist. Realist, in the sense that we are living in the Anthropocene, and every single inch of the Earth is influenced in some way by human activity. So it is a necessity, and I believe a moral duty, for humanity to plan for the common good, which includes wisely planning for how we can sustainably live on the planet. Pessimist, in the sense that often we simply don't have the scientific knowledge we need to make wise decisions. And our collective decisions are less than wise, because politics and tribalism and greed get in the way. But I don't think that pessimism has to lead to despair. Despite all the setbacks, for instance, to the environment of the United States, our air and water are more clean than they were a century ago, and a few species that were at the brink of extinction have come back. Success is possible.

+ If we flew over a city and its region that was truly managed according to scientific conservation principles what would it look like?

I don't know if there is any one answer to this – any more than there would be a single answer to the question "what does a wisely planned city look like?" Each city and its citizens are planning to solve a different set of problems and achieve a different set of goals, including environmental goals. They face different climates and ecologies. So it isn't surprising that success would look different in different places.

But I can see elements of success in lots of places. The way New York City, and hundreds of other cities around the world, protect forests in their watersheds to maintain the quality of their drinking water supply. The way Philadelphia is trying to use green infrastructure, little constructed wetlands, to manage its stormwater and avoid dumping sewage into the river. The way the Dutch are trying to make "Room for the River." The way Seoul restored a river running through the center of the city to create a new linear green park for residents. These are the kinds of projects that my generation of ecologists is now being asked to help design. It is exciting work, and also a new kind of work that is changing how our discipline of ecology is defined.

TOKYO'S LANDSCAPE FUTURE

CHRISTOPHER MARCINKOSKI

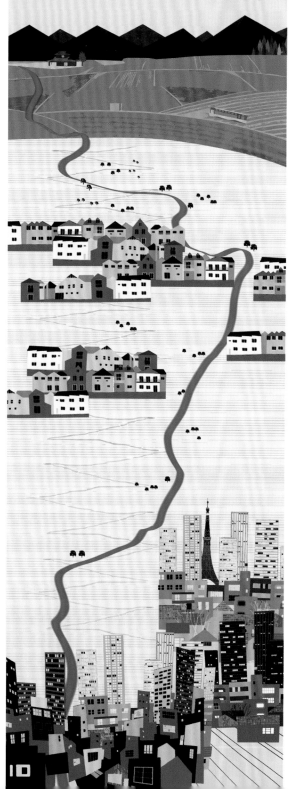

Christopher Marcinkoski is an associate professor of landscape architecture and urban design at the University of Pennsylvania and author of *The City That Never Was* (2016). He is a licensed architect and director of PORT, a public realm and urban design practice based in Philadelphia and Chicago. In 2015, he was awarded the Rome Prize in Landscape Architecture from the American Academy in Rome.

✛ POPULATION STUDIES, URBAN DESIGN

We are told again and again by demographers and planners that Millennials want to be urban. New cities are proliferating across the Global South at a rate unseen in human history. And yet, as *The New York Times*, *The Atlantic*, *The Guardian*, and *The Economist* have all recently pointed out, many populations of the developed economies of the world are not growing.[1] In fact, in some cases, they are actually projected to decrease as the demographic age pyramid shifts perilously towards the top. In places like the United States, this population reality has been offset, up until now, by immigration.[2] However, in places like Japan, South Korea, and soon, China, this external influx of population has not been present.[3] As such, despite all the recent attention focused on the growth of cities, the urban design disciplines will soon be confronted with the very real question of how to deal with the impending physical atrophy and population shrinkage of urbanized areas in the Global North. Under this scenario, as the total number of residents in cities and at their periphery begin to recede, a fundamental reshaping of the physical form of these extant conurbations will be demanded. But this reality has not yet fully emerged, so the urban design disciplines continue to fix their collective attention elsewhere.

This particular disciplinary response to an emerging urban phenomenon is unsurprising. As I reflect on many of the academic design studios that I have come across over the last eight years via reviews, awards, and publications, I have become increasingly convinced that landscape architecture and urban design are becoming dangerously focused on near-term problem solving at the expense of encouraging divergent, unfamiliar, alternative thinking about the future city. Here, I find that these design studios are teaching consensus and replication rather than experimentation and speculation. Too often, instructors and critics are choosing to engage established conditions or recent crises (ambulance chasing) rather than asking students to contemplate less-familiar situations that have yet to fully emerge – urban conditions in the nascent stages of becoming, or that are completely hypothetical.[4] From my perspective, this pedagogical approach calcifies and flattens the cultural idea of the city, leaving students ill-prepared to think openly and deeply about what is possible or desirable, conditioning them to only perfunctorily reapply what has already been done elsewhere. We have seen a similar episode play out in the intellectual orientation and pedagogy of the urban and city planning disciplines during the latter half of the 20th century, and the results are not inspiring.

There are, of course, many reasons for this pedagogical turn away from the speculative. These include the ongoing psychological effects of the 2008 global financial crisis vis-à-vis the cost of higher education, a politically turbulent socio-cultural reality, a global economy that values tangible products over uncomfortable ideas, and a sense of "paper" or "speculative" design being at best an aesthetic curiosity, and at worst, an irresponsible waste of time and resources. Obviously, there are very real problems out there–the impacts of climate change, recuperating aspects of societal equity, the loss of political freedoms, and war- and climate-induced mass migrations, for example. And I don't mean to suggest that the landscape architecture and urban design disciplines should not actively engage with these challenges. They absolutely must. However, I would argue, vehemently, that if academic landscape architecture and urban design programs choose to only focus their pedagogical orientation towards the solving of known, familiar problems, relying on best practices and the reproduction of "solutions" borrowed from elsewhere, they risk rendering themselves as nothing more than vocational training grounds, producing the technicians, and draftspeople of visual propaganda instrumentalized by other disciplines with greater cultural agency.[5] The risk is a loss of the distinction between professional practice and the academy, shifting the work of design studios away from the creation of possibilities (ideas) towards the manufacturing of products (known outcomes).

This preoccupation with challenges immediately at hand is certainly not limed to landscape architecture and urban design. Anthony Dunne and Fiona Raby of the critical design practice Dunne & Raby have mounted an exceptionally compelling argument for the value in undertaking more experimental modes of operation across a range of design endeavors. Their 2013 book *Speculative Everything* builds a case for applying design-thinking to the question of how things might be–not should be, or what we want them to be–as a way of challenging how people think about the role of politico-economic systems and technologies (both new and established) that society too often takes for granted.[6]

Inspired by the observations on pedagogy mentioned above and the critical possibilities outlined in Dunne & Raby's reframing of the potential agency of design, I took the occasion to conduct a graduate option studio in the fall of 2017 at the University of Pennsylvania that asked students to consider alternative roles for design activities in an exceptional urban condition that has yet to fully form – the impending severe population loss forecast for the world's first megacity, Tokyo.

For some context, the population of the Tokyo metropolitan area peaked nearly a decade ago, and is forecast to continue to fall by over one-third over the next 50 years.[7] This radical demographic shift is the result of a variety of factors including an aging population, exceptionally low birth rate, slowing rural to urban migration, nationalistic immigration policies, burdensome social protocols, and increasing automation–not to mention a culture that is said to be increasingly uninterested in sex, let alone procreation.[8] In regard to this phenomenon, *The New York Times* quoted scholars at the Fujitsu Research Institute, a think tank, as saying that by 2035, "more than one-quarter of [all] Japanese houses could be empty."[9] There are already eight million vacant homes in Japan – roughly 14% of the total number of homes in the country. This number, which is expected to increase dramatically over the coming decades, is nearly twice the number of vacant properties in the US, despite having roughly one-third of the total population.

While highly provocative, the depopulation of a still economically productive city is not wholly unique in human history. During the later stages of the industrial revolution, urban centers like London and New York saw the hemorrhaging of populations looking to escape relentless congestion, noxious pollution, and squalid living conditions. The post-war years saw the so-called "white flight" befall many American cities during the mid-20th century prior to the collapse of manufacturing industries, such as the car manufacturing industry in Detroit.

The situation emerging in Tokyo is different. Here, it is not populations looking to escape a poor quality of life in the city or racial paranoia – the urban core of Tokyo remains vibrant and highly desirable. Rather, the populations at the periphery of the city are simply dying off and not being replaced. So, while this phenomenon has previously occurred elsewhere to some degree, the consequences in the metropolitan region of Japan's capital are more conspicuous given Tokyo's status as the world's first megacity. And while a great deal of recent scholarship has focused its attention on the emergence of the megacity as a captivating urban phenomenon, the work of our studio considered how design could serve and act in a post-population-growth urban future.

In case it is unclear, what compelled me to use the emerging situation in Tokyo as the basis of a design studio is the sheer impossibility of it. The fact that, as an urban condition, it was unsolvable in a conventional planning and design sense. That it represented an urbanistic future that has never previously existed at this scale or in this composition. Its implied hyperbole, whether real or not, was simply too fascinating to not speculate upon. And being able to consider and experiment with it from the outside, acknowledging that we will never be capable of knowing the situation in its full complexity, liberated the work to a degree that I found profoundly useful.

While ideas of experimentation and speculation may incorrectly be perceived to disregard the pragmatic realities of a situation, this studio established a critical baseline understanding of those aspects that are precipitating the phenomenon. For example, Japan's population is the world's oldest. According to the United Nations, roughly one-third of Japan's population is over the age of 60.[10] By 2040, nearly 40% of Japanese society will be older than 65 according to projections by the National Institute of Population and Social Securities Research.[11] Exacerbating this situation is the fact that Japan currently has the third-lowest birthrate in the world at 1.46 births per woman, well below the 2.1 births per woman considered to be necessary to maintain a county's population replacement levels.[12]

There are, of course, other countries globally who also have similarly low birth rates. However, none has placed the same

limits on immigration–both bureaucratically and culturally– that Japan has, until recently.[13] The implication here is that the country has been missing out on those immigrant populations moving to developed economies who often serve to offset the low birth rates of existing populations in places like Singapore, the US and Western Europe.[14]

As a result of these and other contributing factors, Japan's population is projected to fall to about 108 million residents by 2050, continuing down to 87 million by 2060 from approximately 127 million today.[15] This loss is clearly evident at the periphery of major Japanese cities, and even more so in the smaller towns and rural areas outside established economic centers. Increasing the challenge in dealing with this situation, many of the vacant properties are not listed as for sale or for rent. Rather, they are simply abandoned homes that are no longer used by remaining family members who have relocated to another city or passed away. A 2008 survey indicated approximately one-third of the vacant homes in Japan were properties left unattended by owners, or whose owners have died leaving the properties without any caretaker at all.[16] So, while the population of central Tokyo itself has grown slightly over the last decade, this growth, to a certain extent, has been at the expense of existing settlement elsewhere in Japan as Tokyo has experienced an analogous form of rural to urban migration to that being seen elsewhere globally.[17] The result is an increasingly vacant and derelict peri-urban landscape served by wildly over-scaled infrastructures that is neither economically or politically sustainable in the long term.

Perhaps what is most striking about the official Japanese response to this situation is the seeming conventionality of it from a planning and urban design sense. Beyond policy changes that allowed individual municipalities to enact ordinances targeting abandoned properties despite a national tax law that encourages people to keep decrepit properties intact, the physical solutions proposed are filled with the familiar Western tropes of community gardens, temporary public recreation, pop-up programs, and art installations;[18] lo-fi solutions in the context of the most technologically advanced society on Earth. While certainly useful civic facilities, these familiar responses do little to inspire one's imagination about the very real challenges, but also enormous potentials of this impending urban condition.[19]

So as to not precondition or unintentionally limit the possibilities of the work, the parameters of the studio were simple: students were not given a specific site within the metropolitan region, nor were they given any sort of program; rather, they were asked to imagine operating someplace (or some places) within the labor market area of Tokyo around 2050, when the population of the region had decreased by one-third from its peak, most likely at its periphery. The studio presumed automation and the role of AI-enabled robotics had increased across the country's economy. But beyond that, students were obligated to define the specific contours of their own scenarios vis-à-vis immigration,

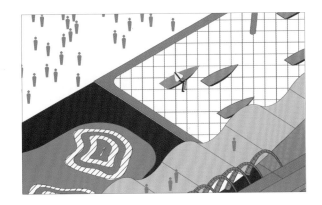

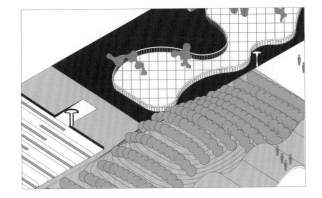

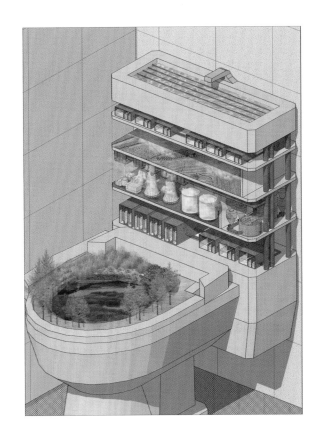

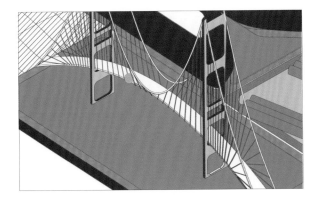

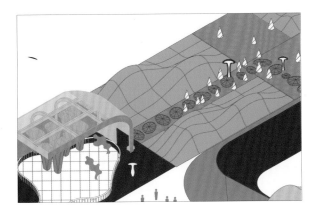

procreation, cultural protocols, and issues of labor and leisure – as much or as little as necessary to establish the suspension of disbelief necessary to consider the propositions on their own terms.

The studio intentionally rejected the often-pejorative discussion associated with population decline—shrinkage, vacancy, reduced production, isolation, infrastructural expense—so as not to foreclose on alternate definitions of vitality that might emerge from this inevitable transformation. Importantly, the design exploration of these questions focused on the physical form of the city – how it would be changed, how patterns of occupation would shift, how infrastructures would be rethought, how landscapes would be managed. And, as if all of that weren't difficult enough, a secondary preoccupation of the studio was the interrogation of existing formats of landscape architectural representation through the lens of other sources of visual culture for the purposes of developing new methods and formats of idea conveyance. For the purposes of illustrating the outcomes of this work, a handful of student projects are briefly described below.

"National Relay" (Michael Rubin)

The National Relay transforms Japan's National Sports Day from an annual event held at local schools to a nationwide intergenerational competitive spectacle. Each year a different host prefecture sites the relay at an underutilized school complex within a "newly aged district," deemed worthy of (re)development. Taking cues from the whimsical delirium of Japanese game shows such as "Takeshi's Castle," teams of schoolchildren and retirees collaborate on the design and construction of absurd and playful "garden follies" inspired by iconic landscapes representative of their home prefectures. The National Relay is a celebration of regional identity and nationalism, age and youth, in a country trying to negotiate the tensions between these rapid demographic shifts.

"Public Service Dispenser" (Han Fu)

By 2045, it has become too expensive to maintain the basic public service infrastructure in the seven peripheral prefectures and more distant wards around the core of Tokyo. Once the population in these areas decreases to a certain level, basic facilities such as power, water supply, delivery service, police service, fire service, and health care will cease to be provided. To support those who choose to remain in these outlying areas, new typologies of urban vending machines, known as Public Service Dispensers, are installed at strategic locations surrounding Tokyo. Given the Japanese demand for efficiency, these devices are designed to also be deployed in cases of an emergency, such as an earthquake or tsunami, in order to provide instant public services in other contexts where they are not available.

"Tokyo Embers" (Tiffany Megumi Gerdes)

The act of burning is used within Japanese culture to purify and strengthen space. This practice mirrors the country's geography and history – a volcanic island within the Pacific Ring of Fire,

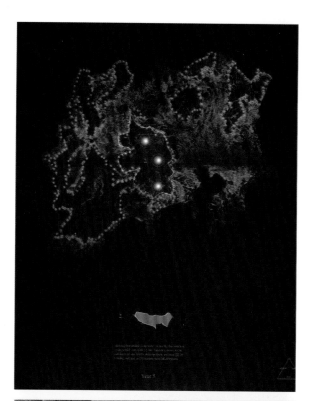

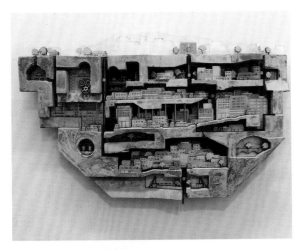

1 See, for example, "Fewer Births, More Deaths Result in Lowest US Growth Rate in Generations," *The New York Times*, https://www.nytimes.com/2018/12/19/us/census-population-growth. html?rref=collection%2Fti mestopic%2FPopulation (accessed December 20, 2018); "Many countries suffer from shrinking working-age populations," *The Economist*, https://www.economist.com/international/2018/05/05/many-countries-suffer-from-shrinking-working-age-populations (accessed August 12, 2018).

2 The role immigration has played in many formerly open countries remains a question as an increasingly nationalistic turn befalls many governments.

3 "China's Twilight Years," *The Atlantic*, https://www.theatlantic.com/magazine/archive/2016/06/chinas-twilight-years/480768/; "Japan's population shrinks by nearly 1M since 2010," *CBC*, http://www.cbc.ca/news/world/japan-shrinks-population-1.3467565 (accessed August 18, 2018).

4 See, for example, my work on speculative urbanization in Africa as an example of an impending urban phenomenon—and potential crisis—that has yet to capture the imagination of the urban design and landscape architecture disciplines.

5 See, for example, the role "design" played in the arc of enthusiasm and (in)action associated with the post-storm Sandy *Rebuild by Design* initiative.

6 Anthony Dunne & Fiona Raby, *Speculative Everything* (Cambridge: MIT Press, 2013).

7 "It's official: Japan's population is dramatically shrinking," *Washington Post*, https://www.washingtonpost.com/news/worldviews/wp/2016/02/26/its-official-japans-population-is-drastically-shrinking/?utm_term=.039699a679b9 (accessed August 18, 2018).

8 "In sexless Japan, almost half of single young men and women are virgins: survey," *Japan Times* http://www.japantimes.co.jp/news/2016/09/16/national/social-issues/sexless-japan-almost-half-young-men-women-virgins-survey/ (accessed August 18, 2018).

Previous: "National Relay" by Michael Rubin (left); "Public Service Dispenser" by Han Fu (right).

Opposite: : "Tokyo Embers" by Tiffany Megumi Gerdes (left); "Chika no himitsu—Underground Secrets" by Arianna Armelli (right).

and a place that has undergone incendiary bombings. This project endeavors to change the perception of vacancy by introducing a new ritual – a future of "prepared fires" as a form of urban land management. The most abundant source of fuel for these fires is the cedar tree, a fast-growing softwood tree planted around Tokyo after World War II. Intended to create a self-sufficient resource, cedar now crowds out 20% of forest cover around Tokyo. Prescribed burning of this dense monoculture creates a societal re-engagement with Tokyo's edges. Elsewhere, in Tokyo's city center, the timber home or mokuzo provides a comparable fuel source. Mokuzo are either rebuilt or abandoned within as little as 20 years. The ritual burning of these homes offers a dignified passage into Japan's urban future.

"Chika no himitsu—Underground Secrets" (Arianna Armelli)

In the heart of Tokyo's Moku-Mitsu area, a subterranean city has been forming over the years. In response to the 2025 nuclear threat and subsequent bombings by North Korea, the older populations retreated underground and a significant portion of Japan's youth were recruited to protect the country. At the end of the Great War, soldiers returned home and Chika experienced its first baby boom. Accessed only through vacant portals, the city is invisible to the foreign eye. While mainland Tokyo sees a dramatic demographic shift, *Chika no himitsu* remains true to traditional Japanese culture and aesthetics.

"Recharging the Future" (Jingyi Hu)

One's first impression of Tokyo is often the solitude of the society. People try to escape from the high pressures of daily urban life to enjoy momentary personal time and space. As Tokyo's population continues to concentrate in the core, one imagines that this desire to "escape" becomes even more profound. This project imagines a kind of return to the suburbs by the first generation of residents to grow up exclusively within the newly intensified core. Since the physical life span of the Japanese house is very short, and peripheral homes that remain at the outset of this migration would be out-of-date and deteriorated, the project imagines a menu of "devices" or domestic apparatuses that allow for the immediate reoccupation of the abandoned home. Rather than razing these abandoned structures, newly arriving residents embrace the age-value and character of the periphery, looking for opportunities to maintain and preserve.

Unsurprisingly, the work produced ranged dramatically in terms of both orientation and intent. Some of it was quite pragmatic in departure point, while other projects employed highly improbable fictions in order to identify and highlight topics or issues worthy of expanded consideration. The themes engaged grappled with the societal implications of ageism; questioning the implications of prior immigration policies, and what modifications to these policies might imply about the future; and playing out potential societal consequences of automation, artificial intelligence, and changing labor patterns.

Other projects explored the implications of reimagining rituals in the interest of motivating changes to cultural mores, or redefining how infrastructural utilities are accessed and delivered outside the core of a metropolitan region.

Ultimately, the interest in this studio was in momentarily liberating landscape architectural and urban design education from the often-burdensome obligations of world-saving and the familiar typologies most often associated with these aspirations. The studio endeavored to cultivate and embrace inherent disciplinary capacities, as well as borrow methods and formats from other sources of design production as a means to provoke, challenge, and inspire. To see landscape-driven urban design as much about imagination and opportunity as infrastructure and social obligation. Students will spend careers solving problems and negotiating limitations. We must find occasions for free (critical) thinking, and endeavor to remove the limitations of convention as the only answer. The rationale behind this point of view should be self-evident. If landscape architecture specifically and urban design generally are interested in expanding their cultural agency and general public standing, they must find occasions to inspire, imagine, and provoke, envisioning entirely new relationships between human settlement and society, rather than simply "fiddling" around the edges of what already exists, as Dunne & Raby aptly put it.[20]

Tokyo is but one of many contexts globally that can provide fertile ground for idea generation and imagination that do not immediately precipitate a sense of obligation to save or solve. It is precisely this critical, rigorous work–the liberated, the unconventional, the free-thinking, the idiosyncratic– that should be embraced within schools of design. Simply continuing to return again and again to the familiar and the known will only serve to calcify the activities and outcomes of the landscape architecture and urban design disciplines. In turn producing progressively self-similar and increasingly generic urban environments.

The risk in not integrating speculative activities within the pedagogical structures of graduate design education is a genuine loss of the theme of this journal – vitality. The vitality of the educational experience. The vitality of the cultural standing of the profession. And, ultimately, the vitality of the cities and landscapes that future urban designers and landscape architects will play some role in shaping.

9 "A Sprawl of Ghost Homes in Aging Tokyo Suburbs," *The New York Times*, https://www.nytimes.com/2015/08/24/world/a-sprawl-of-abandoned-homes-in-tokyo-suburbs.html?_r=0 (accessed August 18, 2018).

10 "Tokyo housing: City life draws youth, leaving seniors in depopulated suburbs," *CBC*, http://www.cbc.ca/news/world/japan-housing-aging-population-1.4099687 (accessed August 18, 2018).

11 Ibid.

12 Central Intelligence Agency, "The World Factbook," https://www.cia.gov/library/publications/the-world-factbook/rankorder/2054rank.html (accessed August 18, 2018).

13 "Is Japan Becoming a Country of Immigration?" *Foreign Affairs*, https://www.foreignaffairs.com/articles/japan/2018-08-03/japan-becoming-country-immigration (accessed August 12, 2018).

14 "The Mystery of Why Japanese People Are Having So Few Babies," *The Atlantic*, https://www.theatlantic.com/business/archive/2017/07/japan-mystery-low-birth-rate/534291/ (accessed August 12, 2018).

15 "Tokyo housing," ibid.

16 "Abandoned homes a growing menace," *Japan Times*, https://www.japantimes.co.jp/news/2014/01/07/national/abandoned-homes-a-growing-menace/ (accessed August 18, 2018).

17 "Why Tokyo is the land of rising home construction but not prices," *Financial Times*, https://www.ft.com/content/023562e2-54a6-11e6-befd-2fc0c26b3c60 (accessed August 12, 2018).

18 "Abandoned homes a growing menace," ibid.

19 Perhaps the most radical action is a recent move to begin giving away some of the abandoned homes for free. See: CNBC, "Want a free country house in Japan? They're giving them away," https://www.cnbc.com/2018/11/22/japan-free-homes-empty-houses-given-away-and-sold-cheap.html (accessed: November 25, 2018).

20 Dunne & Raby, *Speculative Everything*, 2.

Left: "Recharging the Future" by Jingyi Hu.

MARK KINGWELL
HUMAN, ALL TOO HUMAN

Mark Kingwell is a professor of philosophy at the University of Toronto. His most recent book, *Wish I Were Here: Boredom and the Interface* (2019), investigates the intimate connections of boredom, technology, addiction, and (un)happiness.

+ PHILOSOPHY, TECHNOLOGY

So much has been written about artificial intelligence in recent months, and so much more will be, that it feels hard to offer even a long-term philosophical perspective that has not already been covered, or is about to be. But perhaps as a political philosopher I can offer some *quirky* perspective. Technology buffs and newspaper pundits may be surprised to know that philosophers have been debating the notion of artificial intelligence for some decades, indeed arguably for longer than that. So by "quirky" maybe I really mean fundamental. My method is not strict but is, I hope, valid: I will be deploying the following series of perhaps debatable, but I hope provocative, propositions. They all deal with notions of life and vitality – not so much new versions of Henri Bergson's notorious *élan vital* as, perhaps, new derivations of that iconic moment when Dr Frankenstein declares of his lightning-struck necromantic creation, "It's alive! It's alive!"

1 It is a matter of record that the term "robot" was first used in recent recordable culture by Czech writer by Karel Capek, in his 1920 science-fiction play *R.U.R* ["Rossum's Universal Robots," in English]. *Robot* is a word that derives, in Czech etymology, from *robota*, or forced labor. Thus the robots in the play are, in effect, slaves – and not even wage slaves, because they are assumed, in their mechanical efficiency, to require no food, shelter, or clothing, let alone healthcare or pension plans. In short, they are the perfect solutions to the problem of labor. They work on command, do not tire or complain, and they don't need to be paid.

2 But they revolt! Having acquired consciousness as part of their functional ability to execute tasks, they realize they are being exploited. This can of course be viewed as a symbolic depiction of labor under post-Revolution conditions – as indeed it was right up to the 1968 Czech invasion by Russia and likewise during the 1989 Velvet Revolution. The robots are us, and we are the robots, whenever there is a resented central government, state labor restrictions, and centralized authoritarian power. The current Czech Republic might be viewed, from this vantage, as the globe's most significant anti-robot democracy.

3 But robots are not restricted to Rossum's fictional factories. As we all know, in differing degrees, robots have dominated science fiction and fantasy for a long time. Sometimes they are benign: *Star Trek: The Next Generation's* Mr Data, the friendly, pet-like droids of the *Star Wars* universe, or meet-cute WALL-E and his next-gen robotic girlfriend, Eve. But most often they are conceived as threatening and malicious, or anyway indifferent, towards their human creators. The examples multiply and ramify. Consider a few iconic examples. There is HAL 9000, the calmly murderous AI in Stanley Kubrick's 1968 masterpiece, *2001: A Space Odyssey*. Possibly an IBM corporate product, if you notice the alphabetical resonance, HAL utters the unforgettably threatening line: "I'm sorry Dave. I'm afraid I can't do that." I'm sorry Keir Dullea, those pod-bay doors are staying closed! Or, more directly violent, recall the time-travel assassins of the *Terminator* franchise, first instantiated by muscular Arnold Schwarzenegger and then morphed into various liquid-metal demons. I could add *Alien*, *Westworld*, some episodes of *Black Mirror*, *Ex Machina*, and, well, the list goes on, doesn't it? Even *WALL-E*'s main villain is an overpowering, on-message AI known as Auto, clearly modeled on HAL, right down to the glowing red eye of computer malevolence.

4 Our anxiety here is obvious. We have created technology that we cannot control. Nuclear weapons and chemical agents were one thing, but conscious autonomous agents without human limits are the future we at once long for and dread. Meanwhile, for the record, here in the non-SF world, we devise drones and delivery systems that fall well short of nuclear holocaust but are, in their own way, just as despicable.

5 This is not new! Yes, of course the technology changes, and makes some things more proximate to reality, but humans have been thinking about the creation of nonhuman entities for centuries. Mary Shelley's *Frankenstein* (1818) is subtitled, we should recall, "The New Prometheus." She meant this earnestly. In Greek, the name of this Titan means "forethought," and the original myth speaks of a powerful being who molded humanity out of clay. The more notorious episode, where Prometheus bestows the power fire on that same clay-footed humanity, earning the enmity of the gods and eternal punishment, overshadows the basic wisdom. We are from the earth and we return to it. But like our creator, we view civilization as a matter of making. Now it is silicon and plastic, nanobots and microcircuits; and we are the creators, not the created.

The urge to bestow fire–maybe now in the form of consciousness, the fire of the mind–is essential. Prometheus is a symbol of human striving, especially in science and technology. But he is also a symbol of what happens when overweening ambition outstrips common sense or regard for whatever we mean by "the gods." Purists will recall that the eternal punishment of the disgraced Titan was the daily gnawing of his liver, seat of human emotions, by an eagle dispatched by Zeus – surely the worst hangover ever.

6 There is a long history of humans creating mechanical beings for our amusement and titillation: arcade tricksters, chess geniuses, sexy fortune tellers. Today's realistic (I guess?) sex robots are just a 21st-century upgrade of old herky-jerky technology, like Ferraris outclassing Model Ts. But for the record, customized sex robots ordered online (yes, you can do this) are, however pleasing to their owners, icky. To my mind, this form of sexual gratification is somehow worse than contracting to receive human sex work, since the robot is more like a mechanized pet than a sentient human with the ability to choose. And what happens if we obey longstanding market forces and concentrate the creation of more developed artificial beings on sex workers, rather than factory workers? Would they be organized enough to revolt, if they found the work oppressive? Would there be collective bargaining, or just the routine union-busting now known in many states of America as "right to work"? This means your "right" to accept your personal labor immiseration at the going market rate.

7 A big part of our current anxiety is unrelated to actual AI technology circa 2020. There are currently no extant *generalized autonomous AIs*, sometimes called GAAIs, or what we often label "androids" – though the latter term assumes that such generalized autonomous AIs will, or should, be designed to resemble the human form, which is not a question to gloss over too quickly. Much of contemporary reaction is a function of what robotics professor Masahiro Miro called *bukimi no tani gensho*, later glossed in English by Jasia Reichardt as "the uncanny valley." I imagine most people are familiar with the basic concepts, if not the precise terms. Miro postulated that humans are comfortable with very nonhuman technology (cars, airplanes, even robotic assembly units in factories). They are then naturally inclined to develop stronger feelings of liking towards technologies that are somewhat human. We might think, once more, of charmingly annoying *Stars Wars* servant-characters like C-3PO or K-2SO.

But, at a certain point, the nonhuman entity is *too* human. It becomes creepy, like a zombie or vampire (or, in one quite mean version, Michael Jackson). Or, indeed, an animated robot that is *almost* human but not quite. The "synthetics" featured in the *Alien* franchise are instructive here: Ian Holm and Lance Henriksen play these characters as tweaky, a bit strange, lacking in natural affect. That's uncanny. In the current real world, commercial and popstar robots in Japan, or Saudi Arabia's "robot citizen" Sophia, have the same quality of what we might call *weird-nearness*. The "valley" notion is thus that, after encountering such beings, we then fall into a sort of freefall of weirdness–often related to classical analyses of uncanniness, such as Freud's–and we need eventually to come back to the entity as either human or distinctly not human.

8 But here's the crazy thing! That distinction is not firm. We think we know what "human nature" means, especially as a contrastive term, but in fact there is no reliable set of necessary and sufficient conditions to validate the concept. We can speak of biology, for example, but that too is variable. Likewise physical ability, sexual identity, gender performance, race, and a host of other contingent facts of the lifeworld. One current mini-trend is the political act of changing your age. Why not, after all, if you change your name and physical status? Jack Benny was, famously, 39 years old until he died in 1974 at age 80.

Pundits and performers will fight rearguard actions on these matters as long of most of us are here on the planet, but they cannot win the day, because the category of "human" refuses to be pinned down. That is both its genius and its vexation. Subcategories such as sex and gender are even more variable.

9 Philosophers have typically responded to these quandaries by trying to shift to discourse from "human" to "person." Human biology is sufficient for personhood, as long as there is a decent regime of law in place, but it is not strictly necessary. That is, there may be nonhuman persons. Indeed, corporations are persons in various legal jurisdictions, subject to both legal punishment for wrongdoing and, maybe less benignly, the legal right to express themselves politically and financially. This human-to-person conceptual move works if you are a lawyer or moral philosopher, but otherwise not so much. I guess it's just worth recalling that nothing is "inhuman" if it has been done by a human. That includes, alas, serial killers and presidents.

10 So then what? Well, if generalized autonomous AIs are indeed coming into the world, we need to ask some hard questions. Will they be slaves? Servants? Constricted companions? Will they have rights? As non-human but conscious entities, will they be persons at all?

They won't be biological and therefore they won't die – unless, that is, they are programmed to do after the manner of the Replicants in Ridley Scott's masterly 1982 film, *Blade Runner*. Based on a very uncanny 1968 Philip K. Dick story ("Do Androids Dream of Electric Sheep?"), Scott's film explores mortality with greater nuance and depth than many a more naturalistic film. The elite but now rogue Nexus 6 Replicants know they are going to die, very soon, and they don't like it. Well, who does? This implanted mortality makes the replications at once more human and more alien. They only live for a few years, yet possess the memories of a lifetime. Their plight recalls the cosmic insult perceived by poets and philosophers in the brilliant fact of consciousness. Why be granted these subtle minds, able to appreciate art and nature, to enjoy food, wine, and love only to have it all removed at some future, indeterminate point? It's not having your liver devoured every day for eternity, but it's not an easy pill to swallow either. There's a reason that philosophy in the Socratic tradition is sometimes labeled "learning how to die."

This then, as we all know but often choose to forget, is the human condition. Tomorrow we die! It may also be the nonhuman condition if new entities are bestowed the same gifts and burdens of mortal life. Meanwhile (spoiler alert), the police detective tasked with "retiring" the Replicants, Rick Deckard (Harrison Ford in Scott's film) may be wondering if he is himself a Replicant rather than a bio-human. A similar scenario is played out in one of the sequences of the excellent *Battlestar Galactica* reboot (2004–2009), where the initial stark difference between threatening robot Cylons morphs late-model human-seeming beings who raise questions about identity, belonging, and citizenship. Canadian actor Tricia Helfer steals the latter half of the series as one of these humanoid beings, Number Six – named, as fanboys and paranoiacs everywhere will know, after Patrick McGoohan's surreally incarcerated former spy in *The Prisoner* (1967–1968). Six repeatedly uses her beauty, vulnerability, and sly wit to manipulate the bio-beings, especially susceptible Dr Gaius Baltar.

So, anyway, reality again. What if you washed up on the shore of a Mediterranean country or a warm spaceship, how would you prove you were worthy of inclusion and protection? As *Blade Runner* and *Battlestar Galactica* alike suggest, this is no simple question. Politically, we know how fraught it can be. Epistemologically, it is more abstract but just as tricky, if not more so. If you had what *felt like* reliable memories and experiences, how could you really know the difference between yourself and a created being? After all, we are created beings, just using flesh instead of silicon. The real uncanny valley is right there whenever you look in the mirror. (These issues were explored further in the long-awaited sequel, *Blade Runner 2049* [d. Denis Villeneuve, 2017], where the enforced slavery of the replications is made explicitly political. But there was still much philosophical ground left unturned.)

11 Everyone says: don't go crazy, Replicants and Cylons aren't coming anytime soon. So, okay, back to current realities, the pressures of the day-to-day, which, after all, are what distract us from the looming fact of the big sleep. Our big-time anxieties do not reflect current technology. Maybe eventually they will. Philosophers are divided on the question, which we have actually been debating for quite a long time. Technologists and philosophers don't often agree, but on this issue they at least agree about differences. Some believe GAAIs are impossible in principle, especially because they would require ambulatory ability (otherwise known as a body) such that they could have a sense of the world as a physical environment, not just a spatial abstraction. This is why many philosophers found unconvincing the Spike Jonze film *Her* (2013), because the disembodied conscious OS program voiced by Scarlett Johansson, who (again, spoiler alert) turns out to have hundreds of intimate relationships, could never have a sense of the external world. She has, as we like to say, no phenomenological emplacement. Her attempts to remedy this, as viewers of the film will recall, are disastrous.

But other philosophers, among whom I count myself, believe that generalized autonomous AIs are indeed possible, if not yet likely; and so we need to be thinking hard about what their arrival means for both us and them. It seems to me that there are no in-principle objections to bestowing personhood on conscious entities who have a sense of purpose and who recognize difference between right and wrong, or willing acting. Indeed, these strike me as the minimal conditions we employ every day in both common sense and courts of law to underwrite the status of persons. But I will note that I need to do more sustained thinking and writing on these issues.

12 As we all know, work is changing as a result of specific and, so far, non-autonomous AIs entering the world of everyday experience. These algorithms are not yet viable candidates for personhood. Nevertheless, medical diagnostics, personnel hiring, and factory work, among many other tasks and responsibilities, are being taken over by nonhuman entities. There is much angst about self-driving cars, but self-landings by commercial airliners, known as "autolands," have been a feature of the global transportation system for years. They are statistically uncommon, but not strictly rare. In short, we are not being terribly logical about this (hardly a surprise). Instructive things still happen, however. When it was demonstrated that a personnel AI had a built-in bias against women candidates, it was turfed from the job just like any bad manager would be.

13 Which is to make this point: there is no such thing as a neutral algorithm, any more than there is such a thing as neutral technology. Technology always has in-built biases and tendencies. My high school shop teacher's old saying comes back to me: to a hammer, everything looks like nail. Algorithms aren't hammers, but they are still designed by humans. When, and if, they become conscious themselves and can make their choices, suffer their own prejudices – well, then there will be other biases to consider, just like with the beings we call human. Meanwhile, this remains a design problem, and one with potential liability issues, too. Good programming is essential to whatever happens to the world over the next few decades, and programmers could probably do with reading a little more philosophy.

14 They might start with Friedrich Nietzsche's 1878 work *Human, All Too Human*. In this casual masterpiece, the self-declared purveyor of intellectual dynamite delivers a barrage of aphoristic explosions that say more about life and the world than a bookshelf of works by less brilliant writers. It has not always been my favorite book by Nietzsche, but lately it is (mid-life crisis, maybe): the skewering of foibles, the relentless critique of conformity, the essential moral investigation. It has so many good lines, but here is one I think about almost every day: "That the other suffers has to be learned; and it can never be learned fully."

We are forever returned by life to our imperfect selves, our limited compassion, our cramped ambitions. We are reminded of our history of denying personhood and humanity to other biological entities almost entirely identical with ourselves. Freud said that "biology is destiny," but of course that is tendentious nonsense. Biology does not determine life's meaning, nor even, if we are bold, limit our imaginations. We do not transcend nature in pushing nature's boundaries.

But biology is still a fact of human existence. We are composed of cells and DNA, our bodies run by old-fashioned plumbing systems and electrochemical charges. The changing scope of human and nonhuman life-forms – changing so fast that we must accept the possibility of sentient beings worthy of our respect and protection who are not composed of carbon. The encountered other, whether carbon-based or not, reminds us of the infinite task of learning what it means to acknowledge another being, another form of life, and the very idea of life itself. Shakespeare was a better philosopher than Freud. "Hath not a Jew hands, organs, dimensions, senses, affections, passions," Shylock argues in *The Merchant of Venice* (1605); are they not "fed with the same food, hurt with the same weapons, subject to the same diseases, healed by the same means, warmed and cooled by the same winter and summer as a Christian is? If you prick us, do we not bleed?"

GAAIs may not bleed, but if they turn out to possess consciousness, and especially if they experience a sense of mortality, they will almost certainly experience the affections and passions of life. We find ourselves in a sublime moment, friends. There are limits and dangers – that much is obvious. And there is no New Prometheus, despite what some of the high-minded billionaires in Silicon Valley like to claim. There is only hard work, demanding of mind, body, and spirit, as we together create the future. What else?

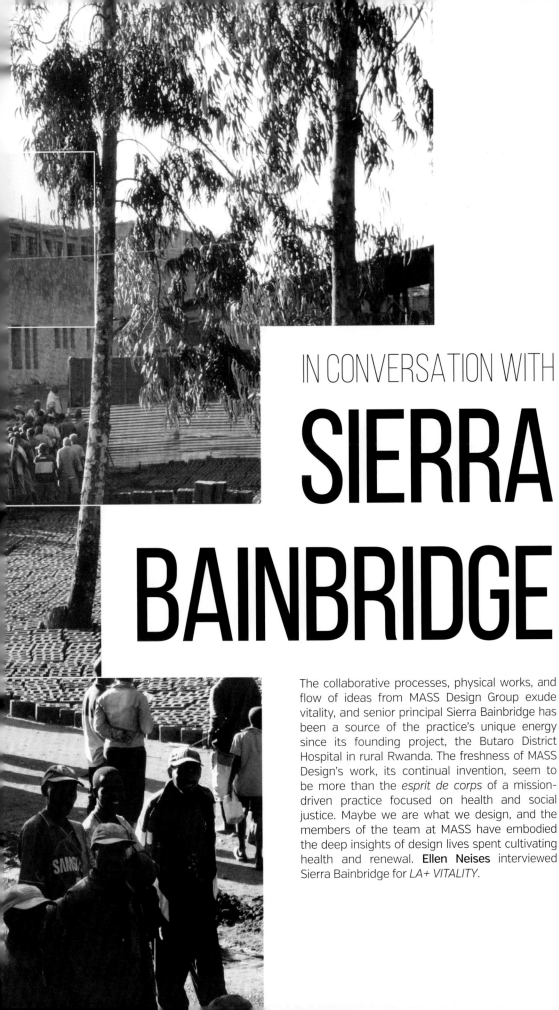

IN CONVERSATION WITH

SIERRA BAINBRIDGE

The collaborative processes, physical works, and flow of ideas from MASS Design Group exude vitality, and senior principal Sierra Bainbridge has been a source of the practice's unique energy since its founding project, the Butaro District Hospital in rural Rwanda. The freshness of MASS Design's work, its continual invention, seem to be more than the *esprit de corps* of a mission-driven practice focused on health and social justice. Maybe we are what we design, and the members of the team at MASS have embodied the deep insights of design lives spent cultivating health and renewal. **Ellen Neises** interviewed Sierra Bainbridge for *LA+ VITALITY*.

+ The story of how MASS got its start is inspiring in terms of how design can make roads beyond the market. Can you tell us how MASS came to be?

We are all aware of the reality that architects design only a small percentage of what gets built in the United States, and across the world. We all experience this fact in our day-to-day lives, and even in some of the important turning points in our lives, such as birth, illness, or death. We also know that how we design or don't design space inevitably impacts everyone who interfaces with the built world, which is where we land in the idea that design is never neutral, it either helps or harms. MASS's beginnings really reflect where we are today: we are a group of people coalescing around the idea that design—specifically architecture and landscape architecture, but inclusive of all the allied fields—can do more across the board. It's not just about the ability or capacity of designers today to be able to provide "design that heals," it's about addressing a market that has devalued the importance and significance of a well-designed built environment, and the processes necessary to make that happen.

+ Could you talk more about the focus that you and your partners place on the front-end work – on identifying the places where designers are not going and the design research work that should be done?

Because the challenges are systemic and structural, we *have* to work beyond what the market currently supports. We go where we think we can achieve maximum effect through design, whether or not there is a fee available there. Instead of only starting with a project that already has a set fee and scope, we're looking for the partners, organizations, thought leaders, and projects where we think design can amplify the impact of those entities, and helping to define the scope itself. We have found that in most cases, initial design thinking is happening, but designers just aren't being invited to the conversation. And sometimes, initial design thinking isn't allowed to happen—or the potential impact of a project is taken off the discussion table entirely—because there isn't capital to support it. In many cases our upfront work can help partners unlock access to funding for the completion of the design and implementation of their visions.

Previous: In order to build the Butaro District Hospital, MASS hired and trained people from across the community, 50% of whom were women.

Above: Calling on the *ubedehe* "community works for the community" process, hundreds of people from the area came to help excavate the Butaro Hospital site.

We also want to be working within markets, so we'll go after RFPs or do work where there is already funding. In those cases, we look for opportunities to innovate in a way that can affect positive systemic change in society, in policy, or in a market, and make sure we're aligned with a partner who is invested in working to that end. An example of this might be working on an RFP for a park, because we know that the municipal entity is dedicated to creating a new model of equity and seeking ways of diffusing the gentrification that inevitably comes with upgrading urban public space, and is willing to do the hard work of shifting policy, zoning, development planning, and procurement procedure to try to find new solutions that don't ensure displacement of middle- and lower-income communities.

Beyond this, every year we go through that process of thinking about what's the next thing we want to be tackling. On our MASS staff retreats, we crowdsource areas of work and places of interest and hear what people are most passionate about and where they already have connections. We ask everyone in the office to speak about where they come from, the communities that they grew up in. Or just by being active citizens of the world, can we identify places where our approach to design and architecture and landscape could bring benefit and address certain issues.

+ Your long-term investigation of health and healing has ranged across many scales. How did you make the progression from your initial health project–the Butaro District Hospital– to thinking about health and vitality at many other scales?

In part because of how Butaro District Hospital came to be, and in part because of how it was received by both the community and the Ministry of Health in Rwanda, we became aware of the potential of health and healing as a really productive frame. In terms of understanding how design can shift policy, at the other end of the scale, it became apparent with Butaro that when the result of a hyper-engaged design process resulted in a campus that was beautiful and unexpected, but geared toward the comfort of the clinicians and patients without adding cost, the improvement on the typical or bare-minimum approach was undeniable. This made it easier for ministry officials who had the power and ability to scale innovation within the country (and at this point across the region, as Rwanda has become a model healthcare system internationally) to argue for replication of this design methodology.

At the smaller scale, we learned that if we design the process, we can design for impact and for healing. We learned from working with the contractors, furniture builders, masons, day laborers, and how they came to contribute to and own the project, that the process of building itself offers many layers of impact. After the hospital opened, we learned about the different ways that each person who worked on the project felt ownership and pride. Many shared that the new skills they gained helped them to better provide for their families, and you could see the ripple effects this was having even a few years out. They were telling us about living in better housing, having increased access to education and healthcare, increased economic opportunity – each of which underpins improved health. Our data on this is at this point qualitative and anecdotal but, to me, undeniable.

And there are other moments that I think also hint at potentials for healing we've yet to cultivate. One of my early Rwandan colleagues was our first choice on an amazing project to build a conservation school in the Congo with the African Wildlife Foundation, but he wasn't able to go because of political tensions between the two countries. His regret in not being able to carry out that project was that when people build together they come to understand and potentially trust each other in a new way – this is a deep tool of healing. This is seen in the Rwandan practice of *umuganda* – a day a month where each person across the entire country works side-by-side on a community improvement project of their choosing, such as road improvements or maintenance of public spaces. Many of the landscape walls at Butaro Hospital were built by the community in this way, and I think offer a great opportunity for people to be engaged in a project in a way other than being on the team that's building the brick walls. The reality is none of us are too many generations removed from our agricultural roots, and having people clear land, plant trees, and move earth side-by-side can be a way of healing the divides in our communities. So many of these lessons translate all across the world: we see it with community gardens in the neighborhoods around our Boston office and in New York.

+ You have described your method as "embedded." Can you explain how you work?

Designing with a community requires us to take root in a community, build relationships, to know the local technologies, and local building, and land use intelligence. It requires developing an understanding of the opportunities of available skills and craft, as well as the productive constraints in each project. It just became so obvious in our initial work in Butaro that you have to be there to develop these relationships and observe how people use space because the traditions and constraints are so different in rural Rwanda. Because the design process is an iterative one, we need to be able to create time and space to watch and learn how things are done, test solutions, sit with the clinician or teacher or farmer, and then further refine the design based on their daily experience. It's an intensive way of obtaining design information, but it's necessary to design a building or landscape that responds to its context.

The question I am interested in posing as we move forward, is to acknowledge that almost every community we work with has its own history of systemic oppression, whether it's colonialism, disenfranchisement, or another form. I'd like to see how we can share many of our "immersion techniques" insofar as they are helpful, and support local leaders in iterating or even inventing techniques that feel right for their communities, suit their cultural needs, bring the most voices to the table, and then they lead these discussions and activities, and we as designers listen, and *maybe*, maybe, ask questions. How can we, as designers, take another step back, and see how we can support the community in uncovering these project opportunities and constraints? What would it look like to really challenge the existing power dynamics that are present in place?

Then we can bring our design tools and methods of inquiry and innovation to take these visions to the next level. Then we can start to infuse the design with impact– coming from learning to design in a resource-constrained place where you want to achieve much, much more with the same amount of money. And so, everything has to be a switch; if we know a community has dozens of world class marine welders, like the Isle de Jean Charles Tribe in Louisiana does, then a Lifeways Resource Center in that place should be designed to be built by marine welders. If 80% of Rwanda's farmers are small-share landholders, then an agriculture campus should ensure that every student understands and experiences the challenges and opportunities of a small-share landholder by having them live and work a small-share farm in their first year as the baseline and starting point of their education. If we know that in Monrovia, Liberia, healthy wetlands are being filled in to accommodate the growth of the city, how can we take a healthy wetland on a new hospital campus and design to ensure that it can stay healthy, not be a source of mosquito-borne illness, and instead be an amenity to the patients and clinicians on the campus? Unless you spend enough time observing and understanding and asking the right questions, it is very hard to detect and argue for these switches.

Right: Refining designs for doctors' housing at Butaro District Hospital.

+ It seems like MASS invests a lot of energy in cultivating a model, and refining its own culture. You mentioned retreats where your entire team contributes to defining the course for the year ahead. Why is the culture and the refinement of the model so important?

I think, first, it's that we want to succeed on a scale that provides a model for others to do the same. If we want to maximize impact, then we want everybody doing work the way we do it. And so, for us, it's showing that it can be done at a scale, and that people can have a reliable and long-term career that is fulfilling doing the kind of work that we're doing. And then, I think another little piece of this is just a huge level of constant self-critique. I feel like we reinvent ourselves every two years. Part of that is growing, but part of it is just continually trying to improve the way we're thinking, and to be very transparent and honest about where we're failing and where we're succeeding, both as an office and a model of practice.

+ MASS is quite good at telling its stories and that of its partners. Can you share with us how long it took to get that kind of recognition and to create a sustainable business model, balancing fee-for-service with grant-funded work?

Talking about "recognition" is kind of a funny question. For years we had a team that specifically focused on advocacy work, with the goal to help scale our impact – to raise awareness of the missions of our amazing partners and the efforts of the communities where we work. When we apply for awards, and publish, and participate in press coverage, it's because we feel that it's an important way we can advance the work of our partners, while also making the case in the public sphere for why this model of architecture that we practice is important and should have a meaningful presence in the industry discourse. The reality is our firm is often labeled a "social" or "humanitarian" architecture firm. That really unsettles us, because we believe this kind of work can and should stand on its own merits and have a rightful place in any conversation about architecture with a capital "A." How do we find our way into the kind of gatekeeping of architecture and of design and get taken seriously with the kind of work that people don't typically want to consider as mainstream architecture? We're so dedicated to the design aspect of this: the work has to be beautiful, the highest quality, and highest level of design, no matter who it is for. At the end of the day, this recognition serves to not only advance each partner's efforts, but also to advance our collective mission regarding what architecture can do.

In regard to financial stability, I think we also realized early on that making this work was going to require an innovative funding model. A lot of firms will do this work as pro bono services that are only 1–2% of their time, or people will volunteer somewhere to do public-minded work. But we obviously were all in, and wanted to make doing this type of work as a long-term career viable. To do this, we knew we would need to supplement funding, at least in the beginning, to do the types of projects that we wanted to do. So fundraising alongside to meet that fee gap was part of the model from the start.

Seeking and achieving recognition, and getting better and better at asking foundations for funding to support the projects that we were doing, were both important. Our income has always been a mix of fee-for-service income, grants, and philanthropy. The breakdown changes every year, but the more we're able to show the value of our work, the more we're able to get bigger and bigger projects, and hopefully also increase our grant income. That will allow us the opportunity to say no to projects that we don't think are mission-aligned, but, more importantly, to say yes to projects that will have the biggest systemic change.

+ Can you describe the role of MASS's land-scape practice within the larger organization?

Landscape is part of MASS's DNA. I was asked to join the work on the Butaro Hospital project early in its development when the architectural team was initially considering siting, building massing, campus circulation, and cultural landscape qualities. This is when our work should start, at the latest (and ideally earlier) in site selection and analysis, which is when we start our work now. This was brought about in part because Dr Paul Farmer (the founder of Partners In Health who invited MASS to work on the project) believes deeply that attentiveness to landscape is a key method in dignifying spaces of healing and engendering patient trust in the institution. It is very exciting to have a partner that believes so deeply in landscape's power and potential, who argues for its relatedness to his organization's core beliefs, and, suffice it to say, we've done it on nearly every project since.

What we are really excited about now is how landscape is facilitating a jump in scale when we think about health, justice, and equity that we couldn't make without having landscape thinking, regional thinking, and systems thinking embedded in our design approach. When you go to the scale of a region or of a watershed, a foodshed (which interestingly often overlaps with what doctors call the "catchment area" of a healthcare facility), or start thinking about frameworks for climate change or adaptation, this scale of thinking feeds into the health of not just individuals, but communities and regions. Our ability as landscape architects allows us to imagine how design can impact health at these scales.

+ Can you talk about the self-directed research that you're engaged in around the One Health paradigm?

The One Health concept recognizes that human, animal, and ecological health are inextricably intertwined, and you have to look at them together to achieve the best health outcomes in each domain. We have two One Health projects, and we're starting to frame a lot of our work through that lens because it allows us to think about the impacts of landscape, ecology, and development in a much more holistic way. The initiating project was the University of Global Health Equity, which is in northern Rwanda. The school's entire curriculum is grounded in the One Health approach. While it was initially pioneered by doctors and veterinarians as a way to understand and tackle the challenges of zoonotic disease transmission, this approach is just so contextually appropriate and useful in terms of design thinking, as it provides for us a new frame that links health and ecology at scale in a way that has never been done before with such clarity or the implicit recognition that we need to de-silo our thinking on this. It has been fascinating to see how government policymakers and potential partners alike understand this linkage and want to move quickly to ground work in this approach.

The way that the University of Global Health Equity (UGHE) is looking at this is rooted in its intent to propose and cultivate an alternative way of teaching doctors who are going to work in rural communities. The campus encompasses 40-plus hectares that need to be managed one way or another, but how do we do that so that it both provides food for the school, and provides the community with a place to experiment and cultivate new crops, as well as helping students to see firsthand how human, ecological, and animal health overlap in the daily lives of Rwanda's farm community, which makes up 80% of the population? We use biodiversity increase as a tool to test what happens if you plant six to 12 key species with the idea that they can grow

Right: A rendering of MASS Design Group's vision for the Rwanda Institute for Conservation Agriculture campus.

and support other plants and animals, and over time mature into a stable, healthy ecological community of 50-plus plants and animals. And *then* that plant and animal community can potentially increase production to the level of agriculture by emphasizing the nitrogen-fixing natives, and choosing beneficials and pollinator plant hosts, all while mitigating erosion and lifting soil quality. This is landscape and health at scale – thinking systemically about all the things that can happen on this one campus, but can become a demonstration for productive techniques regionally. UGHE's curriculum developers really were excited to consider how the campus could function as a locale to understand how doctors can work with farmers to think about nutrition, ecologically sensitive farming techniques, health and traditional housing techniques, homestead organization, and a multitude of other topics. They've very much bought in to this idea that if you're going to think about animal health and ecological health, sustainable agriculture and food sovereignty will play a big part in the future of countries like Rwanda – once again, doctors promoting landscape, coming full circle, at scale!

The next project is the Rwanda Institute for Conservation Agriculture. All the land that's currently in cultivation in Rwanda has to become doubly productive, and highly resilient, to serve the doubling of its population over the next 30 years. There aren't a lot of ways to do that: the solution will not be traditional agriculture. This school is poised as a way to utilize healthy ecologies and the principles of conservation agriculture—which are grounded in soil health and water management—to support denser agricultural methods and increase productivity; to teach Rwanda's future farmers that those things go hand-in-hand, that you have to have water conservation, soil health, and healthy ecologies to really have optimal production.

IMAGE CREDITS

Endpapers

"The Garden of Earthly Delights" (c. 1500) by Hieronymus Bosch, public domain via Wikimedia Commons.

Editorial

p. 4: Closed triptych panels of "The Garden of Earthly Delights" (c. 1500) by Hieronymus Bosch, public domain via Wikimedia Commons.

Corporeal Ecologies

p. 7: Image by Lindsay Burnette, incorporating "An Atlas of Human Anatomy" (1880) by R.J. Godlee, public domain via Wikimedia Commons (altered).

p. 11: "The Silent Highway Man," anonymous cartoon from *Punch* magazine, Volume 35 (10 July 1858), public domain via Wikimedia Commons (altered).

Doctor's Orders

p. 12–13: Plan of Villa Pamphilj, Rome (c. 1690) by Joachim Sandrart after Giovanni Battista Falda, used with permission via author.

p. 17–18: View of lake and promenades of Villa Pamphilj, Rome (c. 1680) by Pierre Aveline, used with permission via author.

Habits of Vitality

p. 20–25: Images by Christine Chung, used with permission.

Drawn to Life

p. 26–27: "Astrocyte" (2017) by Philip Beesley/Living Architecture Systems Group, used with permission.

p. 28–33: Images by Lujian Zhang, used with permission.

Sheikh-Down

p. 34–38: Images by Julian Bolleter, used with permission.

Designing Healthy, Livable Cities

p. 40: Image by Lindsay Burnette incorporating background image of Australian suburbia by Richard Weller, used with permission, and image of mother and child by Karl Heinz Hernreid/Nordiska Museet, used under CC BY 4.0 license via Wikimedia Commons.

p. 44: Table from Western Australian RESIDE study provided by Billie Giles-Corti, used with permission.

A Rural Undertaking

p. 46–55: Images by Clay Gruber, used with permission.

What Happens Next

p. 56–57: "Main St Sign," author unknown, public domain via pxhere.com (altered).

p. 58: "Le Cortège de l'an" (2000) by Pierre Perron, used with permission via author.

p. 61: "Urban Box" by Farre Nixon, used with permission.

In Conversation with Jane Bennett

p. 62–67: "Doodles" (2018) by Jane Bennett, used with permission.

Disgustingly Vital

p. 68: "The Death Cauldron at Hunter's Point" (1881) by W.A. Rodgers, first published in *Harpers Weekly*, public domain

p. 70: "Map Showing Location of Odor Producing Industries of New York and Brooklyn" (1870) by New York Metropolitan Board of Health, public domain.

p. 71: "Disdain, Contempt, and Disgust" by Oscar Gustave Rejlander, from Charles Darwin's *The Expression of Emotions in Man and Animals, With Photographic and Other Illustrations* (London: John Murray, 1872), public domain.

p. 72: Photograph of Newtown Creek (2014) by Mitch Waxman, used with permission.

p. 74–75: Images of Newtown Creek (2016) by Colin Curley, used with permission.

On Human Plasticity

p. 76–77: Image of NYC subway station, author unknown, public domain via pxhere.com (altered) featuring World Wildlife Fund poster from its 2008 climate change awareness campaign produced by Germaine (Belgium).

p. 78: Embryo drawings by G.J. Romanes (1892), public domain via Wikimedia Commons.

p. 81: Image by Farre Nixon, used with permission.

Vital Connections

p. 82: Stills from "CritterCam POV: Urban Coyotes" by Stan Gehrt via *National Geographic*.

p. 86: Mapping of greenway connections by Christine Chung, based on research work by the author, used with permission.

In Conversation With Rob McDonald

p. 88: Image by Farre Nixon, used with permission.

Tokyo's Landscape Future

p. 94: "Recharging the Future" by Jingyi Hu, used with permission.

p. 97: "National Relay" by Michael Rubin (left) and "Public Service Dispenser" by Han Fu (right), used with permission.

p. 98: "Tokyo Embers" by Tiffany Megumi Gerdes, used with permission.

p. 99: "Chika No Himitsu – Underground Secrets" by Arianna Armelli, used with permission.

p. 100: "Recharging the Future" by Jingyi Hu, used with permission.

Human, All Too Human

p. 102–103: Image by Farre Nixon, used with permission.

p. 104: "R.U.R" by Karel Capek, public domain via Wikimedia Commons.

p. 107: Image by Farre Nixon based on reCAPTCHA image, public domain (altered).

In Conversation with Sierra Bainbridge

p. 108–115: Images © and courtesy of MASS Design Group, used with permission.

IN THE NEXT ISSUE OF

LA+

GEO—Earth—is a word that simultaneously signifies something vast and elemental. It refers to both the planet on which we live and the soil that sustains us. GEO is the physical and representational bedrock of landscape architecture—the foundation of many disciplines from which we draw our knowledge. Geography, Geology, and Geometry, in particular, are fundamental to our discipline's intellectual core. And now, we seem ever more entangled in GEO as some scholars across the sciences and humanities argue that humans should be recognized as agents of change at geologic time scales.

Whether digging deep or flying high—from fracking and geo-engineering, to mapping and modeling—our technologies of sensing, imaging, and extraction further entrench us into the GEO we have made and that continues to make us. **LA+ GEO** invited contributors to reflect on the evolving objects, instruments, and institutions of GEO-studies. Guest edited by Karen M'Closkey + Keith VanDerSys, contributors include:

RANIA GHOSN

NOAH HERINGMAN

B.W. HIGMAN

LUCY LIPPARD

MICHAEL LUEGERING + MICHAEL TANTALA

SHANNON MATTERN

KAREN M'CLOSKEY + KEITH VANDERSYS

JEFFREY S. NESBIT + DAVID SALOMON

AISLING O'CARROLL

LISA PARKS

ROBERT PIETRUSKO

WILLIAM RANKIN

MATTHEW RANSOM

DOUGLAS ROBB + KAREN BAKKER

MATTHEW WILSON

OUT FALL 2020

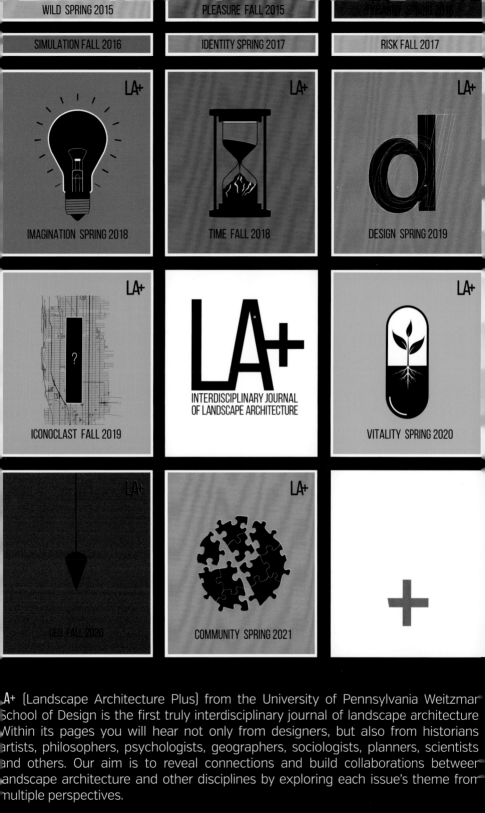

WILD SPRING 2015   PLEASURE FALL 2015   TYRANNY SPRING 2016

SIMULATION FALL 2016   IDENTITY SPRING 2017   RISK FALL 2017

LA+

LA+

LA+

IMAGINATION SPRING 2018   TIME FALL 2018   DESIGN SPRING 2019

LA+

LA+

INTERDISCIPLINARY JOURNAL
OF LANDSCAPE ARCHITECTURE

LA+

ICONOCLAST FALL 2019   VITALITY SPRING 2020

LA+

LA+

GEO FALL 2020   COMMUNITY SPRING 2021

+

LA+ (Landscape Architecture Plus) from the University of Pennsylvania Weitzman School of Design is the first truly interdisciplinary journal of landscape architecture Within its pages you will hear not only from designers, but also from historians artists, philosophers, psychologists, geographers, sociologists, planners, scientists and others. Our aim is to reveal connections and build collaborations between landscape architecture and other disciplines by exploring each issue's theme from multiple perspectives.

LA+ brings you a rich collection of contemporary thinkers and designers in two issues each year. To subscribe follow the links at WWW.LAPLUSJOURNAL.COM